D1601571

SCHEMERS & DREAMERS:
FILIBUSTERING
in
MEXICO
1848-1921

SCHEMERS & DREAMERS:
FILIBUSTERING
in
MEXICO
1848-1921

JOSEPH A.
STOUT, JR.

TEXAS CHRISTIAN UNIVERSITY PRESS
Fort Worth

Library of Congress Cataloging-in-Publication Data

Stout, Joseph Allen.
  Schemers and dreamers : filibustering in Mexico, 1848-1921 / Joseph A. Stout, Jr.
    p. cm.
Includes bibliographical references and index.
  ISBN 0-87565-258-1 (alk. paper)
  1. Filibusters—Mexico—History. 2. Mexico—History—1821-1861. 3. Mexico—
History—1867-1910. 4. Mexico—History—Revolution, 1910-1920. 5. United
States—Foreign relations—Mexico. 6. Mexico—Foreign relations—United States. I.
Title.
  F1233 .S87 2002
  972'.04—dc21

                                        2002002778

For
B. J. S.

CONTENTS

PREFACE

The international border between the United States and Mexico is almost 2000 miles long and today is the focus of conflicts between the two countries concerning immigration and illegal drugs. The U.S. government and many *norteamericanos* are interacting more than ever with Mexico and Mexicans, and Mexico rapidly is increasing in strategic importance to the U.S. Between 1990 and 2000 several million Mexicans crossed the border into the United States. Most arrived looking for work, while a few engaged in illegal activities. Many *gringos* view this immigration phenomenon as a threat to U.S. sovereignty and ultimately to the internal security of the country. Illegal immigration, drug smuggling, North American Free Trade Agreement (NAFTA), and growing U.S. business investment in Mexico have prompted an intensifying political, economic, and social dialogue between the two countries. Some individuals in the U.S. have suggested such radical actions for controlling immigration and stopping drug smuggling as permanently militarizing the border with regular U.S. Army troops. Mutual concerns about border problems are presently receiving the kind of scholarly attention deserved in both nations. Today the violators of the international border are coming from the south side of the international line, but historically in the nineteenth and early twentieth centuries the opposite was true as various groups formed north of the border in preparation for entering Mexico.

For many decades scholars on both sides of the line have studied violation of Mexican territory on the part of groups organizing in the U.S. These studies have included filibusters, bandits, cattle thieves, American Indians, and a motley assortment of scoundrels who created problems between the two countries. Historically these efforts have threatened Mexican sovereignty. During the nineteenth century the Mexican government referred to individuals who aimed to invade Mexico in armed groups as filibusters (derived from the Dutch *vribuiter,* meaning pirate or free booty). Adding to the destabilizing activities of armed groups entering Mexico, the United States and several other nations during the nineteenth and early twentieth centuries either intervened militarily or threatened to do so. As a consequence, Mexico lost a great deal of its national territory and has reacted with justifiable paranoia about threats to its security from north of the international border. Some of the relatively small, armed parties that the Mexican government called filibusters actually entered the country hoping to gain a permanent foothold and perhaps annex more territory to the U.S. Other groups recruited and organized publicly to filibuster in Mexico, but never crossed the border. Mexico viewed these threats as a form of intervention in its internal affairs, an attitude derived from Mexico's having lost almost one-half of its territory to the U.S. during the nineteenth century.

Discriminating between filibustering expeditions launched into Mexico, and Mexican-led revolts against their government, has always been difficult for Mexican leaders. Rebellious opposition groups were not filibusters in a traditional sense, although in diplomatic correspondence with the U.S., Mexico usually referred to the actions as such. Whether any plan to enter Mexico was carried out or whether the leaders were U.S. citizens was unimportant to the Mexican government. To Mexico the signficance was that the groups recruited, organized, and planned their entry into Mexico from the United States in full view of the U.S. government, as newspapers in both countries contained dozens of articles about these efforts.

Filibustering is still important to Mexican-U.S. relations today. While it is only a historical curiosity to *norteamericanos,* Mexicans believe that what happened in the past is relevant to present negotiations concerning mutual border problems. Mexicans long have perceived the U.S. as a threat, while the U.S. has often paid scant attention to its neighbor across the Río Bravo.

In 1985 I was flying via Mexicana airlines from Oaxaca to México, D.F., sitting next to a Mexican businessman. I told him I had been to a conference on Mexican history, and he persisted in telling me of the plight of his country in losing so much territory to the United States. At the end of the flight, he suggested rather humorously that Mexico was taking some of the area back through immigration. This example about the importance of a country's history to its contemporary attitudes and actions demonstrates that many Mexicans have been profoundly affected by their history; if one is to understand Mexico and its position in respect to the United States today the past cannot be ignored.

Mexicans see in violations of their borders all the problems they long have suffered at the hands of the United States. Several Mexican historians and popular writers have focused their efforts on the theme of border violations from north of the international line. In 1971 Gastón García Cantú published *Las invasiones norteamericanas en México*, in which he generally discussed United States intervention in all its forms from the nineteenth century until the early twentieth. This work has remained so popular in Mexico that it is in its fifth edition. In 1987 Angela Moyano Pahissa published *México y Estados Unidos: Orígenes de una relación, 1819-1861,* in which she focused on United States intervention and included a brief discussion of filibustering. Luis G. Zorrilla's monumental two volume study, *Historia de las relaciones entre México y Los Estados Unidos de América, 1800-1958*, also contained information about the various filibustering expeditions, viewing them as intervention.[1] In *The United States and Mexico*, published in the U.S. in 1985, Josefina Zoraida Vásquez and Lorenzo Meyer, both distinguished professors at the prestigious Colegio de México, wrote of the importance of the past and the impact it has on United States-Mexican relations today. They suggested that all forms of interventionism and Mexico's loss of half of its territory to the United States in the war of 1846-1848, a conflict Mexicans often call the "War of American Intervention," remains important to Mexicans. The authors also noted that "history still shapes Mexican responses to U.S. actions, but not the other way around."[2] In reference to filibustering in the 1850s they declared that

the expansionist spirit was still very strong, and the local and national U.S. authorities, who were often sympathetic to those who wanted to expand U.S. territory, did nothing to stop the expeditions openly organized in the United States. There were many types of filibusters from small groups of cut-throats who were satisfied with raiding and stealing to those whose goal was to conquer territory.[3]

The authors believed that the cost of *gringo* filibustering was expensive for Mexicans, because *filibusteros* "caused damage, and forced Mexico to spend part of its limited financial resources on defense, which could have been avoided had the famous decree of neutrality been enforced."[4] They wrote that for filibustering the United States accepted "no responsibility, not even in extreme cases like Crabb's filibuster."[5]

Scholars and journalists north of the border also have offered interpretations of Mexico and its relationship with the U.S. In 1989 Patrick Oster summed up the attitudes of Mexicans about territorial loss and interventionism when he wrote in *The Mexicans: A Personal Portrait of a People:*

> Mexicans have fashioned a foreign policy grounded in principles of national sovereignty, nonintervention, and peaceful resolution of disputes. A strange little museum in Mexico City, the Museum of National Intervention, epitomizes this attitude. On long lists on the museum's walls, the government has recorded every violation of its sovereignty — every war, every skirmish, every time two *gringos* stepped over the Rio Grande.

Oster adds that Mexico refuses to forget, and thus "official anger about hundred-year-old military losses and decades-old diplomatic insults smolders as if such offenses occurred last week."[6]

Explaining further some of the attitudes on both sides of the border, historian John H. Coatsworth and political scientist Carlos Rico edited an interesting work, *Images of Mexico in the United States*, in which they suggested that images and perceptions affect the diplomatic decisions of both nations. Often the images are not valid, but are nonetheless important. Coatsworth and Rico believe that "Perceptions (correct or incorrect) of the nature, capacities, and intentions of friends as well as adversaries are important in almost every international exchange or transaction" and that "Culturally conditioned images, even (or especially!) stereotypes, thus exert a powerful effect upon decision-making."[7] None of the above works was based extensively on Mexican documents that deal specifically with filibustering expeditions, but explain in part the attitudes Mexican leaders had and still retain. The focus of these works is generally Mexican-U.S. relations across a broader spectrum of topics.

Historians in the United States also have dealt with filibustering, American Indians, banditry, and revolutionaries who opposed the government and used the U.S. as a base from which to launch raids into Mexico. Some of these topics are analyzed in W. Dirk Raat, *Revoltosos: Mexico's Rebels in the United States, 1903-1923, 1903-1923*; Ward S. Albro, *Always A Rebel: Ricardo Flores Magón and the Mexican Revolution*; Lowell L. Blaisdell, *The Desert Revolution, Baja California, 1911*; and William O. Scroggs, *Filibusters and Financiers: William Walker and His Associates*. Don M. Coerver and Linda B. Hall have studied conflicts focused on the border in *Texas and the Mexican Revolution: A Study in State and National Border Policy, 1910*, and *Revolution on the Border: The United States and Mexico, 1910-1920*. Coerver and Hall dealt extensively with myriad anti-government groups, American Indians entering Mexico on raids, and military expeditions that crossed the border allegedly in pursuit of Indians and bandits.[8]

In diplomatic discussions with the U.S. after 1848, the Mexican government referred to any expeditions formed in the United States as filibustering groups. Often this assessment was correct. *Norteamericanos*, in fact, schemed to filibuster into Baja California immediately after the U.S.-Mexican War. The sentiment for acquiring more Mexican territory by purchase or force remained strong in the U.S. throughout the seventy-three-year period examined in this study. Press reports of efforts to organize expeditions in the United States prompted Mexican protests. In many instances, Mexican diplomats in the United States sent to the Mexican secretary of foreign relations within days of publication articles about filibustering expeditions. Mexicans also read articles published in the United States that suggested Mexicans were incapable of governing themselves. Inflammatory news items, including racial slurs, and the apparent reluctance of the United States to stop filibusters signaled to Mexicans that the United States did not respect them or their sovereignty. Authorities from south of the border could only conjecture that the United States was secretly financing and supporting covert operations through the filibustering attempts. To Mexicans it appeared that when the United States attempted to stop filibustering, it did so selectively and only after evaluating the goals and composition of each group.

To Mexicans it also seemed plausible that the United States supported the ventures for economic, political, or ethnic reasons. Economic investment by U.S. citizens in Mexico increased after 1848, especially on the frontier, and the United States played a central role in the plans of filibusters who sought economic or political and military advantages or annexation of Mexican territory. More often than not diplomatic dispatches from American ministers in Mexico did not reflect a great deal of concern nor sincerity on the part of United States leaders in respect to stopping filibustering. The messages exchanged with Mexican officials, while polite, did not significantly decrease diplomatic tensions on both sides of the border.

Political and social conditions in Mexico and in the United States also encouraged filibustering. Mexico suffered many "revolutions" between 1821 and 1921. During much of the time government stability was so tenuous and volatile that the northern frontier states, left to develop their resources and protect themselves, were vulnerable to the attacks of filibusters, Indians, and bandits, many of whom came from north of the border. Considerable Mexican territory, particularly in the northern states, was thinly populated and underdeveloped. *Peones* who worked on the haciendas, in the mines, and in other labor-intensive occupations earned a pittance, suffered from poor health and diets, had little or no education, and survived with considerable difficulty. Endemic political instability, pervasive corruption, and capricious weather conditions that brought periodic drought in much of the country combined with myriad other problems to plague the nation.

In the United States, politics, war, the press, racial bias, and economics influenced attitudes and desires in respect to Mexico. Some presidential administrations were expansionist, encouraging violation of Mexico's sovereignty. In the nineteenth century U.S. national movements also motivated men to become filibusters. Some erstwhile filibusters had read Moses Y. Beach's or John L. O'Sullivan's writings about Manifest Destiny and the ideas surrounding this phenomenon. Other *gringos*, whether reading about Manifest Destiny or not, were racists in their attitudes toward Mexico. White supremacists believed that only the Anglo Saxons from north of the border could bring stability and modernization to Mexico, a land according to this line of thought, filled with inferior Indians and mestizos. Others north of the border believed that in some fashion Mexican authorities had wronged them or their families, while still others believed Mexico offered opportunity for great adventure or for quick riches. A few men who sought to lead filibustering expeditions also had experienced some economic prosperity in the settlement of the American West, but their good fortune had been temporary, and thus these westerners hoped again to find easy fame and fortune south of the border. Others who talked about and who went through the motions of organizing filibustering expeditions were probably dreamers or schemers imagining the impossible.

Dreams and schemes of conquering Mexican territory lingered in the minds of some men north of the border well into the twentieth century. In 1921, U.S. Senator Albert B. Fall issued his well-known anti-Mexican Senate report, encouraging U.S. acquisition of Baja California or additional territory along the north Mexican frontier. His report again stirred the ambitions of entrepreneurs who talked of organizing armed parties to enter Mexico.

The lasting significance of filibustering relates to Mexico's long-standing attitudes toward the United States and its ability to threaten Mexico with intervention. Mexico's traditional posture of non-intervention in respect to the sovereignty of any nation probably has resulted in part from its experience with the U.S.

Determining just what constituted a filibustering expedition has been difficult, and disagreement exists on both sides of the border. I have decided that those groups organized in the U.S. that were comprised of a large number of or a majority of United States citizens whose aims were to establish themselves permanently in Mexico were basically filibustering expeditions, as were those groups the Mexicans believed to be freebooters, whether led by *gringos*, Mexicans, or individuals from a third country. The most important fact is that the expeditions were organized and departed from north of the border. Motivation was as varied as the leaders' backgrounds. In some instances Mexican nationals hoping to overthrow the Mexican government organized or participated in the expeditions. But many of these Mexican-led incursions were comprised of a considerable number of *gringos* who intended to separate or annex to the United States part of the north Mexican frontier. Often both the Mexicans involved and their *norteamericano* counterparts tried to use each other for their particular aims. Some men, Henry A. Crabb and Juan Napoleón Zerman, for example, claimed that Mexican authorities invited them to colonize. During the Porfirato some people claimed that economic policies and new immigration laws encouraged *gringos* to enter Mexico in order to import capital and to exploit natural resources. In a few instances, the intent of the adventurers was unclear.

It is worthwhile to note that while it was the U.S. that failed to stop illegal armed groups that invaded Mexican territory during the nineteenth and early twentieth centuries, today, in the minds of *norteamericanos* the reverse exists as immigrants and drugs flow freely north across the border. Presently, U.S. authorities believe that Mexico does not do what it should to stop Mexicans from entering the U.S. illegally. The objective of this book is to suggest a partial explanation for present Mexican attitudes concerning border problems by describing the parties Mexicans referred to as filibusters. I hope to show that Mexico's position in respect to their citizens' illegal crossings into the U.S. today is similar, at least in the minds of Mexicans, in many ways to the filibustering era when the U.S. offered that it could do little about border transgressions.

As a consequence of the interest in Mexico concerning filibustering as a form of interventionism, approximately fifteen years ago the archivists at the Archivo Histórico "Genaro Estrada" de la Secretaría de Relaciones Exteriores reorganized, catalogued, and separated the materials relating to filibustering. The documents number into the thousands and can be found in a new index under Fil—and various numbers. The archivists also have attempted to discriminate between genuine filibustering expeditions from the United States and the purely anti-government movements that frequently organized along the frontier.

Many archivists and historians have assisted me during the course of this study. I wish to thank Profesoras Angela Moyano Pahissa, formerly of the Universidad Nacional Autónoma de México, and Ana Rosa Suárez Argüello at the Instituto de José María Luis Mora in México, D.F., for sending me materials. Lawrence Douglas Taylor of El Colegio de la Frontera Norte in Tijuana provided me a copy of his excellent study *La Gran Aventura En Mexico*. Much of the research for this work was done at the Archivo Histórico "Genaro Estrada" de la Secretaría de Relaciones Exteriores (AHSRE), and I owe a debt of gratitude to Licenciado Roberto Marín Maldonado, Jefe del Departamento del Archivo Histórico, and to his competent staff. Dra. Stella María González Cicero, Directora General del Archivo General de la Nación (AGN), Licenciado Jorge Nacif Mina, Director General del Archivo Histórico Central, and Roberto Beristaín Rocha, Jefe del Centro de Referencia at the AGN, have either given me permission to see documents, or assisted me in locating hard-to-find files. Licenciada Patricia Galeana Valadés past director of the AHSRE and the

AGN assisted me in both locations. Archivists at the Hemeroteca Nacional located at the Universidad Nacional Autónoma de México and at the Biblioteca Miguel Lerdo de Tejada also helped greatly. Licenciado Salvador Rodríguez Carrillo, Director de Documentación y Difusión at the AHSRE provided photos, as did Susan Sheehan, photo librarian at the Arizona Historical Society, and Nancy Vélez, Library of Congress. Angeles Magdaleno in México retrieved documents and photos for me.

Several readers in the United States have offered suggestions for revision of the manuscript. I am particularly grateful to Bonnie J. Stout for her support of my research travels and to Paul J. Vanderwood, San Diego State University, who read an early draft several years ago. Don M. Coerver, Texas Christian University, read the manuscript, made numerous insightful suggestions, and sent to me an excellent Mexican quote about Ernesto Dalrymple. I also followed many research trails in Mexico with friends Harry P. Hewitt of Midwestern State University, Douglas W. Richmond of the University of Texas at Arlington, and David Adams of Southwest Missouri State University. I have enjoyed the support of John M. Dobson, Dean of the Oklahoma State University College of Arts and Sciences, and William S. Bryans, Chair of the Department of History. I am especially grateful to Michael M. Smith of Oklahoma State University, my colleague in the history department for thirty years, who has read the drafts, taught me a great deal of Mexican history, and attempted to keep my errors to as few as possible. Any errors. of course, are my own—the result of my learning process about Mexican-U.S. history.

Joseph A. Stout, Jr.
Oklahoma State University
Stillwater

1

ANTECEDENTS

In 1804 at Weehawken, New Jersey, Aaron Burr and Alexander Hamilton faced each other on the field of honor. Shots were fired, and when the smoke from the black powder cleared, Hamilton lay dead on the grass. Burr won this duel, but in doing so he sent his public career on a downward spiral from which there was no recovery. Desperate for some way to stabilize his future, he quickly conspired with the nefarious United States Army Brigadier General James Wilkinson, who told him of a plan he had to take away some part of New Spain and make it an independent nation. Wilkinson, an unscrupulous blackguard, was in the pay of both the United States and Spanish governments.[1] The first filibustering expedition into what would become Mexico appeared about to take place.

Between 1804 and 1806 Burr cast about seeking financial support to put Wilkinson's scheme into motion. By the summer of 1806, President Thomas Jefferson had heard of Burr's plan and that Wilkinson, whom Jefferson earlier had made governor of Louisiana Territory, also was implicated. Wilkinson must have gotten word that information about the plan had leaked out and wrote to Jefferson telling him of Burr's conspiracy. Owing to Wilkinson's duplicity and Jefferson's determination to stop Burr, the plan fell apart. Burr was eventually cleared of any charges of armed intervention into New Spain, as a consequence of Chief Justice John Marshall's insistence that evidence must be presented that Burr indeed had organized a group to enter New Spain. This interpretation established guidelines for United States authorities, who for more than the next hundred years had to contend with filibustering into Mexico.

The desire to acquire more territory on the U.S. southern border began early in the history of the country and did not expire easily. To Spaniards, and to Mexicans after independence in 1821, there had appeared no doubt that the United States government frequently supported the violation of their territory. Spaniards witnessed ample evidence before, during, and after the War of 1812 that American expansionists wanted to annex all Spanish territory in North America. The United States had expressed interest in Florida and Louisiana before 1803. Even before 1800 U.S. citizens had taken up residence between Natchez and New Orleans. Many of these new arrivals looked wistfully at Spanish territory as a fertile field of territorial and political opportunity. President Jefferson had encouraged settlers to enter West Florida, believing that the United States must acquire that region and, at least, New Orleans in Louisiana. And, in this era the United States Congress publicly supported the idea that the U.S. should acquire the two areas "by purchase or conquest."[2] After 1803 the United States justified its actions by arguing that the Louisiana Purchase had included West Florida. On January 15, 1811, Congress annexed West Florida east of the Perdido River. Yet the country's thirst for more territory was not satiated with this acquisition. Now the United States also wanted East Florida. President James Madison contrived clandestinely with several Americans to foment revolution there, while the government prepared to occupy the area militarily. James Monroe, secretary of state, communicated with George Mathews, an adventurer with grandiose ideas of conquest who wished to establish himself in East Florida and annex the area to the United States. Monroe did not support Mathews officially, but neither did he oppose him.

Mathews planned to lead an armed party to East Florida, capture St. Augustine, then ask the United States for annexation.[3] In almost every way Mathews was a filibuster who had the support of U.S. government officials. Mathews organized, incorporated a few Spaniards into his party to make the movement appear to be a local one. Displaying a flag of his design for the new country, he attacked St Augustine, while American naval vessels threatened Spain's small fleet. Once he had succeeded, Mathews learned that Monroe had disavowed any knowledge of the affair, and Mathews headed to Washington to confront the secretary. En route, while resting at Augusta on about September 1, 1812, Mathews mysteriously died.

In 1819 the United States and Spain, in the Adams-Onís or Florida

Purchase Treaty, temporarily resolved the border problem by making East Florida part of the United States and recognizing United States ownership of West Florida. Other provisions included United States' acceptance that no part of Texas had been included in the Louisiana Purchase. With the ink on this treaty scarcely dry, John Quincy Adams, then secretary of state, publicly expressed the view that all Spanish territory on the southern boundary of the United States would become part of his country eventually. The majority of Americans of that generation might not have shared this opinion, but what was important was that this was a view of a high-ranking government official. Spaniards were aware of such attitudes.

Texas provided more evidence of the aggressiveness of the United States and its citizens who thought about adding more territory to the fast growing Union. Between 1811 and 1821 other adventurers from the United States cooperated with Spanish and Mexican nationals to take more territory beyond the international border. In 1811 Spaniard José Bernardo Maximiliano Gutiérrez de Lara and American adventurer and former U.S. army officer Augustus W. Magee led a group into Texas across the border from Nachitoches, Louisiana, but failed to gain a permanent foothold because of Spanish military presence in the region. In June 1819 James Long led an armed party into Spanish territory. Spanish soldiers once again expelled the interloper and his party. Long then joined with another Spaniard and in 1820 they tried to establish a position on Galveston Island and foment rebellion against Spain in Mexico. Both efforts failed, and Spanish authorities arrested Long. In 1821 a Mexican prison guard shot him.

In 1820 Spain had given Moses Austin a permit to colonize a section of Texas. The next year, after Austin's death and the successful completion of the Mexican independence movement, the Mexican government validated the colonization permit to Austin's son, Stephen F. Austin. Austin and others eventually received several *empresario* land grants, recruited eager souls and began the colonization of Texas. The ambitious *gringos* who settled sections of Texas soon found themselves in conflict with Mexican rule. In 1836 they launched a rebellion that resulted in the establishment of the Republic of Texas. Mexico never accepted the loss of its northern province. Adding to the insult, the United States annexed Texas in 1845. In 1846 a two-year war between the nations resulted in more losses when much of today's American Southwest was taken by the U.S. In the minds of Mexicans, this was unequivocal evidence that the U.S. remained a threat to their nation's sovereignty.

In 1844, while the United States debated the annexation of Texas, others who coveted Mexican lands were organizing and launching a filibustering expedition from New Orleans. Francisco Sentmanat, possibly a Spaniard, recruited a motley assortment of Spaniards, Englishmen, and Frenchmen to filibuster into Tabasco, Mexico. On May 27, 1844, the party of approximately eighty men, sixty of whom were Spaniards, left New Orleans on board the American chartered *William A. Turner.* Their aims were unclear, but the fact that they launched the venture from the United States convinced Mexicans that this was a filibustering expedition.[4] Unfortunately for Sentmanat, Francisco de Arrangoiz, Mexican consul at New Orleans, heard of the scheme and advised his government. When Sentmanat and his men reached Mexican waters, they were confronted by two war vessels demanding their surrender. According to sketchy information from Mexico, some of Sentmanat's men were shot, and others were eventually released upon the intervention of the Spanish, French, and British governments. It is said that Mexican authorities severed Sentmanat's head and boiled it in a pot of oil as a warning to others.[5] Although no one seemed to know just what Sentmanat's goals had been, and there were evidently no Americans involved, Mexico still blamed the United States for allowing such an expedition to be organized and launched from its territory.

With the exception of Sentmanat's sojourn, between 1821 and 1848 no filibustering expeditions from the north occurred, although many Americans entered Mexican territory—most illegally. Intervention from the United States into Mexico—in the sense of paramilitary incursions—happened more frequently after the signing of the Treaty of Guadalupe Hidalgo, which ended the war between the countries in 1848. Even in the negotiations to bring the war to a close it became apparent in the U.S. that many people north of the border wanted additional Mexican territory, perhaps all of it.[6] Although President James K. Polk might have at times favored the idea, his desire for Mexican land did not include getting involved in a long conflict. General Winfield Scott's occupation of Mexico City had not resulted in the destruction of the Mexican army, which remained a threat. Contributing to the failure to acquire more Mexican territory was Nicholas P. Trist, Polk's special envoy sent to negotiate a treaty, who remained in Mexico during this period and negotiated according to his original terms that ultimately called for acquisition of more territory. Perhaps more important was the fact that the Whig political party opposed acquiring all of Mexico. Some historians of the war have intimated that had Trist obeyed his orders of October 6, 1847, to end negotiations and had returned to the United States, Polk would have acquiesced to the pressures of his expansionist cabinet and sent a new negotiator who would have insisted upon total annexation. While most Americans were happy to have ended the war as a consequence of Trist's treaty, some still dreamed of taking part of the northern frontier of Mexico by whatever means possible.

By 1848 informed Mexicans were aware of the ongoing desire of many people in the United States to acquire additional Mexican territory. Considering the relations between the two countries it was only natural that the Mexican government viewed with considerable suspicion any discussion in the United States about opportunities to acquire land in Mexico.

2

THE POLITICAL CLIMATE, 1848-1860

In May 1848, Querétaro, Mexico, was a prosperous city of beautiful colonial architecture lying along the main route from Mexico City to the northern frontier. Here the representatives of the Mexican and United States governments congregated to finalize the Treaty of Guadalupe Hidalgo that Nicholas P. Trist had negotiated. Luis de la Rosa, Mexican secretary of foreign relations, Nathan B. Clifford, attorney general of the United States, and Ambrose H. Sevier, chairman of the Senate Foreign Relations Committee, met in a specially prepared building late in May where the Mexican officials hosted a dinner. Everyone was stiffly polite, but the affair did not please anyone.[1]

Mexicans assumed that the U.S. would live up to its treaty obligations and would enforce its neutrality laws in respect to continuing armed intervention. What Mexicans did not comprehend was the peculiar nature of U.S. neutrality laws. The laws permitted anyone to stockpile arms and ammunition as long as they did not use the U.S. as a base from which to launch an expedition into a country that was at peace with the U.S. It was, of course, illegal to organize and arm rebels who planned to attack a legitimate government. Mexicans hoped that strict enforcement of the United States neutrality law of 1818, which prescribed a potential fine of $3,000 and a prison term of three years for violators, would allow Mexico to develop economically and politically without interference.[2] Soon after signing the treaty ending the war, it became obvious to Mexicans that neutrality laws would be hard to define. The problem for U.S. authorities was the difficulty of proving that any organization that appeared to threaten Mexico was anything more than a publicity stunt or a legitimate colonization venture under Mexican laws. Mexicans soon realized that enforcement of the neutrality laws was sporadic and selective.

Complicating matters in the U.S. was the fact that there were too few federal agents in the field who understood the law. The overlapping responsibilities between U.S. agencies, inconsistent and confusing actions of local and state officials north of the border, including federal judges, customs collectors, agents of the Bureau of Investigations, and occasionally the army in policing the border complicated the situation. So much confusion existed on the north side of the border that on many occasions when groups organized in the U.S., no agency monitored their actions.[3]

The Treaty of Guadalupe Hidalgo awarded to the United States approximately one-half of Mexico's territory, including California and present-day Arizona and New Mexico. Mexico agreed to accept its fate in respect to Texas and gave up claims to lands that extended beyond the immediate frontier states. In Article 11 of the treaty the United States agreed to protect the Mexican frontier from any type of attacks originating north of the border. Article 11 was important to the Mexicans. They realized that Indians along the frontier had for centuries raided the region. Mexicans had heard the long-offered United States claim that one of the reasons it wanted the area was so it could protect Mexican and United States territory from the incursions of hostile tribes.

Mexican internal politics were also unstable until well into the regime of General Porfirio Díaz in the last quarter of the nineteenth century and tended to make Mexico vulnerable to outside interference, especially along the northern border. Mexican politics had been characterized since independence by a struggle for power between centralists and federalists. Centralists generally represented the interests of those who wanted to keep government power in the hands of the central government. Included in the group were religious, landowning, and military elites. Federalists were comprised of those who espoused state autonomy in political and economic affairs. Late in 1848 General Joaquín de Herrera, a liberal, became president, but he remained in office only until 1851. In 1851 General Mariano Arista, also a liberal, assumed the presidency, serving until 1853, when Antonio López de Santa Anna resumed the presidency for his last time. During Santa Anna's presidency the United States sought to purchase more Mexican territory; Santa Anna ceded additional Mexican land to the United States for $10,000,000. In the Mesilla Treaty (Gadsden Purchase Agreement) the Mexican president also agreed to the abrogation of Article 11 of the Treaty of Guadalupe Hidalgo.

Liberals were furious and in 1854 in the *Plan de Ayutla* called for Santa Anna's ouster. By November, 1855, liberal forces had deposed Santa Anna and established Juan Alvarez as provisional president; Benito Juárez served as minister of justice and religion.[4] Juárez, interested in reforming Mexican society, quickly alienated the church and the military by reducing their influence. Conservatives launched a counter attack that resulted in Alvarez resigning in December. Ignacio Comonfort, a conservative, assumed the presidency. He soon alienated Juárez and other liberals by not redistributing lands to the peasants. The Ley Lerdo of 1856 had further limited the power of the clergy, but had done nothing else to satisfy the overall demands of the liberals. In addition, liberal-conservative conflicts had contributed to the poor state of readiness of the Mexican army and state militias. The military institutions had failed miserably to protect the country from the U.S. during the war of 1846-1848 as a consequence of their composition, training, poor weapons, lack of individual decisiveness, weak leadership overall, and sectional rivalries. The permanent army and the militia formations were usually under strength and soldiers were poorly motivated. Most soldiers were Indians who had been recruited without any consideration of their abilities and motivations. Those who could be trained provided brave ranks who served well.[5]

In 1857 Mexican statesmen wrote a new constitution, reaffirming the principles of federalism and giving congress considerable powers. Conservatives who opposed any legislation deemed anti-clerical or restricting their power and influence fought against implementation of the constitution and Comonfort resigned. Benito Juárez assumed the presidency on December 1, 1857, determined to carry out the provisions of the new constitution.[6] Conservatives seeking to regain power soon rebelled against Juárez, and General Félix Zuloaga proclaimed himself president on January 11, 1858. What followed was the three-year War of the Reform during which Juárez occupied Veracruz and Zuloaga Mexico City. The United States recognized the Juárez government on April 8, 1859, helping Juárez in his bid to be the legitimate president of Mexico. Juárez occupied the presidency until the French intervention forced him to flee to the northern frontier. Between 1848 and 1857 the frontier often reflected national problems. Difficulties frequently were magnified because the frontier was so sparsely populated—so near the United States yet so far from the central government in Mexico City.

Prominent Mexican statesmen: Mariano Arista, General Félix Zuloaga, Ignacio Comonfort *(courtesy Archivo General de la Nación, México, D.F.).*

National struggles between conservatives and liberals in the frontier states destabilized the area that bordered the United States. The entire region also suffered Indian raids launched from north of the international line and endless efforts by Americans attempting to organize para-military or filibustering ventures.[7] Despite its internal problems during this period, Mexico had attempted to halt, albeit unsuccessfully, incursions into its northern territory from the United States.

During 1848, 1850, 1852, and later in the nineteenth century, Mexico tried to resolve the problem of too few people on the frontier by offering plans to colonize the region. The first was formulated on July 19, 1848, when President José Joaquín de Herrera decreed that military colonies would be established along the border with the United States to act as a buffer against filibusters and Indians. He guaranteed that when the colony had made sufficient progress it would be turned over to civilian control. According to the plan, the frontier was to be divided into three parts: the Eastern Frontier—Tamaulipas and Coahuila; the Middle Frontier—Chihuahua; and the Western Frontier—Sonora and Baja California.[8]

Indians who cooperated and resided near the colonies were to be paid for their support. Each region was to be meticulously organized in military fashion, similar to the presidial plans Spain had used earlier. A colonel would command the entire region and a captain would command individual colonies. Any man who enlisted for service in the military colonies had to serve six years, received a bonus when his enlistment ended, and received title to land near the colony. The Mexican government promised material and financial incentives to encourage civilians to volunteer.

This attempt at colonization failed almost from the beginning. The government established several colonies, but a shortage of settlers and sporadic financing prompted abandonment of most settlements during the administrations of Herrera and Arista. By 1850 only nine of the eighteen colonies scheduled actually had been constructed, and only two of the proposed six on the western frontier were garrisoned. Indian raids soon reduced these two to complete ineffectiveness. In Baja California by the end of 1849 only one colony existed and its men were ready to leave shortly after arriving. The failure occurred as a consequence of too few volunteers and the inability of the Mexican central government to fulfill its guarantees of supplies and assistance.

Sonoran leader General Mariano Paredes presented his ideas for a colonization plan to the Mexican Chamber of Deputies on August 16, 1850.[9] He warned that Indians were laying waste to Sonora, and that the United States was always ready to exploit any opportunity to gain more Mexican territory. He proposed to allow European and Mexican colonists to settle in the north. The Mexican Chamber did not approve this plan, despite its author's careful details and sound argument.

In January 1852 General Juan N. Almonte, an experienced military leader and politician, offered a third colonization plan. Almonte had considerable experience dealing with the United States and did not think that the northern neighbor was an immediate threat. He was more concerned about Indians who attacked from north of the international line. He believed that the Mexican government should sell land to settlers for a small price and give them money to move to the frontier. The Mexican government did not implement the plan.[10] Nonetheless, a considerable number of Mexicans recognized that political instability and economic weaknesses plagued the country, and that it needed to develop the frontier to protect the area from the United States.

Politics in the United States between 1848 and 1860 also were important for understanding what occurred in that country in respect to filibustering and in its relations with Mexico. With the election of Democrat James K. Polk to the presidency in 1844, the nation resumed its expansionist movement.[11] The land-hungry Democrats lost the presidential election of 1848, and General Zachary Taylor, an old Whig, assumed the presidency. Taylor and the men he appointed to cabinet positions were not interested in foreign adventurism and did not believe that the United States needed more territory to develop. Taylor died soon after assuming the presidency, and his vice president, Millard Fillmore became leader of the Whig party. Fillmore was not appreciably more interested in expansion than his predecessor. He warned all adventurers contemplating violation of United States neutrality laws that he would do all he could to stop the outfitting and launching from the United States of any filibustering expedition to Cuba, Mexico, or any other place. Still, filibustering expeditions were planned and some were launched from several sections of the United States during the period of his presidency.[12] Fillmore made little effort to control such activities.

Millard Fillmore *(from the Collections of the Library of Congress, Washington, D.C.).*

Juan Almonte *(courtesy Archivo General de la Nación, México, D.F.).*

Dark horse Democrat Franklin Pierce won the presidential election of 1852, and he did so with the support of the expansionists. In his inaugural address of March 4, 1853, Pierce spoke in favor of United States expansionist policy as one necessary for the growth and security of the country. Pierce, however, soon learned that his time would be taken up not by the question of expansion of the United States into new territories, but by the question of slavery and its growth. He appointed as members of his cabinet both slave and anti-slave supporters, but named expansionists to lesser positions. He designated South Carolinian James Gadsden minister to Mexico, and John L. O'Sullivan minister to Portugal. Both appointments demonstrated Pierce's interest in expanding American boundaries.[13]

During 1854 Pierce's envoys set about to separate Cuba from Spain. At the same time, Gadsden completed negotiations with Mexico for the United States' purchase of 45,000 square miles of territory along the present Arizona-New Mexico boundary with Mexico. Ostensibly the United States wanted the Mesilla Strip, as it was called, so a transcontinental railroad could be constructed through the region. There had also remained a boundary problem left over from the Treaty of Guadalupe Hidalgo. The two countries had not correctly surveyed and marked the international boundary, and this error would eventually be corrected as a result of the purchase. Although the treaty relieved the United States of any specific obligation to stop Indian raids into Mexico, the U.S. had already shown that it was unwilling to station enough troops along the border to guarantee safety on either side.

Because of the difficulties concerning the organization of the Kansas-Nebraska territories and the general mood in the United States, no additional expansion could take place. It is conceivable that if the United States had not been in such a turmoil that the country at least would have acquired Cuba, either by purchase or by some form of encouragement for governmental support of a filibustering expedition. In fact, the crisis of the Union that developed more fully during the administration of President James Buchanan, who was elected in 1856, precluded any official expansion by the United States. Almost all debates and votes in either the United States House of Representatives or the Senate were shrouded in the cloak of sectional controversy. Upon the election of Abraham Lincoln in 1860, the country headed into a Civil War that overshadowed all desire for acquisition of more territory.[14]

3

1848-1855

Between 1848 and 1855, motivated by the political and economic climate in Mexico and the United States, several adventurers in the United States tried to take advantage of the Mexican frontier by organizing and leading filibustering expeditions. Some who wished to lead these efforts were Mexicans disenchanted with their own government, but they recruited their followers from eager North Americans who saw an opportunity like the situation in Texas in the 1830s.[1] Taking advantage of the political violence and controversy on both sides of the border between 1848 and 1855, several adventurers sought to profit. The first violation of Mexican territory occurred not along the United States and Mexican border, but far to the south in the Yucatán. The political and social elites of the Yucatán had wanted to separate from Mexico ever since the nation won independence from Spain, creating an opportunity for adventurous Americans. Mexican authorities vigorously opposed the separatist movement. Some Yucatán citizens unofficially approached President James K. Polk in 1848, asking for help in subduing the rebellious Mayan Indians and fighting against Mexican political control. Polk was sympathetic, but took no action. There were, however, many veterans of the war who were aware of the situation in the Yucatán and hoped to to use it to their advantage.

Joseph A. White and David G. Wilds quickly raised more than 500 men—who were to receive 320 acres of land for their participation—to filibuster into the region. White, who appointed himself colonel, sailed from New Orleans during December 1848, and landed on the coast of the Yucatán thirty-five miles from Mérida. G. H. Tobin, a lieutenant in the group, later reported that the Mayas had destroyed farms and villages and that the American party had fought the Mayas on December 25, suffering twenty-five casualties. Maya leader Jacinto Pat fought a guerrilla war in difficult terrain so successfully that within five days of the battle many of the Americans resigned and left. About 200 men remained to confront the Mayas again near Valladolid, where the Mayas defeated them. The survivors fled the country, arriving at New Orleans on March 13, 1849.

While the Yucatán continued to be attractive to United States adventurers, filibustering more often occurred in the northern frontier states of Mexico because of their proximity to the United States. The first filibustering expedition into the northwestern frontier was that of Joseph C. Morehead, who led his eager party into Mexico in 1851. Morehead was a mysterious individual who claimed to be the son of James Turner Morehead, governor of Kentucky from 1834 to 1836. The Morehead family refused to recognize Joseph, and whether he was related or not cannot be determined. Whatever his origins, Morehead left Kentucky during the Mexican War and accepted a commission as a lieutenant in Stevenson's New York regiment of volunteers en route to California.[2] After the war, Morehead remained in California, where he represented one of the mining districts in the state legislature. He also practiced law and in 1850 Peter H. Burnett, governor of California, appointed him quartermaster general for the state. In this capacity he had access to state-supplied weapons used primarily to fight Yuma Indians. Evidently Morehead did lead a successful expedition against the natives, but decided that an armed body of men might serve needs beyond merely fighting Indians.[3]

On one of the Indian campaigns Morehead conceived the idea of leading *filibusteros* into Mexico. In 1851 John McDougal, the second governor of the state, assumed office and heard rumors that Morehead had abused state power in forcing ranchers to give him supplies for his expedition. Rumors even prevailed that Morehead had engaged in a bit of banditry as well. And, the governor learned, the expedition that Morehead led against the Indians had cost the exorbitant sum of $75,000. After insisting upon an investigation, McDougal learned that there were serious discrepancies in the financial reports concerning the Morehead effort against the Yumas. California issued a warrant for Morehead's arrest, but by then he was beyond reach.[4]

Actually, early in 1851 while still in the employ of the state, Morehead

had recruited in Southern California for a venture into Mexico. By the end
of March 1851, groups of men had passed through Los Angeles to join
Morehead at San Diego. Plans called for invading Mexico by ship and land.
Morehead had acquired the small bark *Josephine* and planned to sail to
Mazatlán. He also acquired another small boat to take men to La Paz in Baja
California.[5] Morehead evidently experienced considerable trouble securing
supplies in San Diego and in fact owed a large sum of money to local mer-
chants who threatened to get their guns and collect. Morehead's troubles
were greater than local discontent. His expedition was slow to organize and
many of his volunteers abandoned the scheme before the venture got underway. Somehow the wily entrepreneur resolved his problems and on May 11,
1851, with forty-five men he boarded the *Josephine* for Mazatlán.[6]

United States naval authorities arrived at San Diego shortly after
Morehead departed, and, assuming he was heading for Sonora, attempted to
locate him. The effort failed. In addition to the bark *Josephine*, Morehead's
other small ship sailed for La Paz about the same time. Newspaper coverage
of Morehead's expedition reached Mexican officials in Sonora far in
advance.[7] On April 19, 1851, Rafael Espinosa advised government officials
that some Americans had already arrived at La Paz. He suspected that they
might be part of Morehead's filibusters, and he vowed to watch them carefully. Seven days later Espinosa reported that he had learned that Morehead
and his party had left San Diego for Baja California.[8]

Morehead was headed for Mazatlán, however, and in late July he arrived
with approximately 200 men. The force was not heavily armed, and upon
seeing that the Mexicans had arranged a hostile reception for them,
Morehead claimed that his party were miners interested in working in
Mexico. Mexican authorities did not believe the story, but decided to take
no action other than expelling all the Americans. Morehead was sent back to
the United States early in August on the Mexican brig *Iturbide*. According to
some participants in the event, a similar scenario occurred in La Paz.
Morehead had also sent men overland toward Sonora, but the Mexicans were
similarly warned of the approach of this group. Near Arizpe, Sonora, the
adventurers learned they were heading for Mexican *Guardia Nacional* units.
They quickly retraced their steps to the United States.[9] Some who were
involved in the Morehead expedition undoubtedly joined other efforts initi-
ated in California during that period. Morehead was reported back in

Sacramento, California, in 1852, allegedly organizing another filibustering expedition. Evidently nothing became of that.[10] The Mexican government protested that the United States had allowed Morehead to organize and launch a filibustering expedition, but the American government merely expressed its concern.

Almost at the same time in 1851, another eager *filibustero* was planning to lead a party into the northeastern frontier of Mexico. José María J. Carvajal enthusiastically recruited Texans for an invasion of Tamaulipas. Carvajal was descended from a prominent Spanish family. His place and date of birth are unknown, although his family had lived near San Antonio, Texas, during the middle of the eighteenth century. In 1823 Carvajal journeyed to Kentucky where he worked as a leather tanner and saddle maker. After two years in Kentucky, he traveled to Bethany, Virginia (now in today's West Virginia), and attended school where he came under the influence of Alexander Campbell, a well-known Protestant theologian. Carvajal renounced his Catholicism and became an avid Protestant.[11]

Carvajal had been a friend of Stephan F. Austin and continued the relationship when he returned to Texas in 1835. Austin helped him secure a job as a surveyor for *empresario* and colonist Martín de León. Carvajal was elected to the Texas-Coahuila legislature in 1835 but encountered difficulty with Mexican authorities. He fled to New Orleans, where he and two others secured a ship. They loaded the vessel with trade goods and ammunition and headed for the Texas coast to begin a commercial venture. A Mexican ship intercepted the men, confiscated their goods, and imprisoned them. Carvajal and his confederates quickly escaped from jail.

Carvajal apparently was involved in trade—mostly illegal—until 1839 when he led a group of American volunteers in an attack against Mexican centralists near Mier. He was wounded in this battle and permanently lost the use of his left arm. He dropped from sight again until 1846, then organized a group of Mexicans to oppose the invasion of the Americans when the war between Mexico and the United States began. After the war, Carvajal resumed trading with Mexicans across the border from Texas. Mexican tariffs were exorbitantly high, so Carvajal and others on both sides of the border, including Charles Stillman, a merchant who had large investments in land and shipping both in the United States and Mexico, smuggled goods into Mexico without paying duties. In 1851 Carvajal and other Mexicans who opposed the tariffs, probably with the financial assistance of Charles Stillman and other Texas businessmen, organized a revolt against the Mexican authorities. In the *Plan La Loba*, Carvajal called for an end to the high duties, the withdrawal of Mexican troops from the region, and the creation of a free-trade zone along the frontier. Carvajal quickly learned that Texans were anxious to support him, although their motives differed. Carvajal avowed publicly that he was the only one who could bring progress and stability to the frontier. Some Texans who joined his movement were interested in opening northern Mexico to trade, while others wanted to separate the north from Mexico and annex it to the United States. In fact, Carvajal entertained a similar idea. He reportedly said that he wanted to create an independent state out of the frontier and call it the Republic of the Sierra Madre. Stillman was a strong proponent of the scheme and had made his feelings known publicly. Whatever Carvajal's intentions, the Texans who volunteered to help him talked openly of the movement as a filibustering expedition.

Between September 1851 and October 1855, Carvajal or Texans claiming to be part of his movement, led several forays into Mexico near Matamoros. Carvajal announced to local newspapers that he planned to create the Republic of the Sierra Madre out of the entire northern frontier. The Mexican government was aware of the plan and stationed troops near the border. Carvajal was well-known on both sides of the international boundary. One newspaper characterized him as the most "miserable freebooter and rapacious robber the valley of the Rio Grande could boast." Another said he was typical of men "who are disposed to engage in any enterprise rather than do hard work, and hence it is that expeditions of this kind are so popular."[12]

Carvajal organized his first *entrada* into Mexico almost under the shadow of the United States Army at Fort Brown, directly across the border from Matamoros.[13] He recruited approximately 300 enlistees for this initial venture. The men eagerly enlisted for three or six months and were allowed to join if they had their own arms, ammunition, and other equipment. Each man had to swear an allegiance to Carvajal and was to receive the same pay as a Texas Ranger. Mexican officials referred to Carvajal both as a *filibustero* and a *pronunciado*, or one rebelling against established authorities. They believed he was trying to gain complete control of the country. The government leaders also believed that Carvajal enjoyed the support of commercial interests on both sides of the border and the covert support of U.S. officials. Finally, the Mexicans were convinced that the United States was saying a great deal about preventing invasions like Carvajal's, but doing nothing to stop them.[14] In fact, the United States was concerned about violation of Mexican territory, but Buckingham Smith, secretary of the U.S. legation in Mexico City, reflected official opinion that Carvajal was simply an insurgent opposing the Mexican government and that his activities did not concern the United States.[15] Smith chose to ignore the fact that many Americans were collaborating with Carvajal.

Officially the United States was trying to stop the ventures, and President Millard Fillmore suggested publicly that such activity cast the United States in a bad light. He threatened violators of United States neutrality with "grave penalties" and ordered Generals P. F. Smith and D. E. Twiggs to make every effort to stop the filibustering.[16] Twiggs told the War Department that he could not help because many of his troops deserted and joined Carvajal when they had the chance. Despite the threats, Carvajal pursued his goals, Texans eagerly joined him, and the Mexican government continued to believe that the United States was not sincere in trying to stop the activities. In November 1851, Mexico protested officially through regular diplomatic channels that filibustering remained a problem.[17] The United States responded that it regretted the activities, but could do nothing more to stop the adventurers, especially in view of Mexico's refusal to allow United States troops to cross into Mexico in pursuit of any group.[18]

In January 1852, José F. Ramírez, Mexican secretary of foreign relations, advised Robert P. Letcher, United States minister to Mexico, that "adventurers" were still recruiting "in the interior of Texas" and were "expected on the northern frontier within a few days, for the purpose of continuing the disastrous war which is being carried on against Mexico." Ramírez added that Mexico was "holding the government of the United States responsible for the evils and expenses which Mexico is experiencing and sustaining for the purposes of defending herself against the enemies of peace."[19] The United States did not respond. In fact, United States officials expressed little concern. They were negotiating for a possible canal across Tehuantepec, but worried that the filibusters might interfere with the negotiations.

Diplomatic dialogue notwithstanding, Carvajal continued his activities and in September 1851, having recruited a sizeable force mostly of Texans, led his party across the Río Bravo. On September 20, 1851, the group attacked and occupied Camargo, which Carvajal entered long enough to pronounce himself liberator.[20] He told local Mexicans that the Texans in his venture were necessary to fight the "blind and barbarous instruments of despotism."[21] After this grandiose proclamation, Carvajal led his men back across the border.

On October 9, with Matamoros as his eventual target, Carvajal again led his army across the border. Former Texas Ranger John S. "Rip" Ford and a party of former Rangers accompanied Carvajal.[22] Mexican generals Don Antonio María Jaureguí, José L. Uraga, and Francisco Avalos marched Mexican troops to oppose the invasion. On October 20 Carvajal engaged the first of the defenders and fought his way into Matamoros. Local Texas newspapers recorded his progress. One paper, demonstrating Texan support and involvement, referred to Carvajal as a "gallant colonel." The paper predicted a fight with Mexicans "which will do no discredit to the defenders of liberty." The same paper believed that "before forty-eight hours lapse, this city will yield to the invincible arms of the liberators." Carvajal earlier had proclaimed that his goal was "to free the people from injustice and oppression; to see extended over my whole country just and equal laws, which will protect the lowest as well as the highest citizens in the life, liberty, and the pursuit of happiness."[23] Whether Carvajal was serious mattered little. Texans who helped him were not particularly concerned about Mexican rights.

The battle for Matamoros proved more difficult than expected. Although Carvajal had approximately 800 men, Mexican general Avalos had 600 troops who established themselves in strong positions on high ground above Matamoros and in the town plaza. Reinforcements were scheduled to arrive at any time. The Mexicans also carefully deployed two artillery pieces, and although they did not have sufficient ammunition, they loaded the cannon with rocks and sprayed the battlefield. Local Texas newspapers referred to the fight as the "Battle of Ceralvo." Despite the tenacious opposition of the well-deployed Mexican troops, Carvajal and his men fought their way into the city, reaching the neighborhood of the main plaza. For unexplained reasons—perhaps he heard of the approach of General Uraga with reinforcements or his old friend General José María Canales (who had signed the *Plan La Loba* with Carvajal but still led Mexican troops) warned him that he was in immediate danger. Carvajal ordered his men to withdraw to the outskirts of the village. The invaders hesitated momentarily, then marched rapidly twelve miles away. Carvajal left a detachment in Matamoros to observe the Mexicans. The rebels were quickly trapped when Mexican reinforcements arrived and all were either captured or killed.[24] Captain John S. Ford criticized Carvajal's leadership in the battle, stating adamantly that the men Carvajal left behind were sacrificed uselessly, and that the battle could have been won decisively if Carvajal had not withdrawn.

When the news reached the United States, another flurry of newspaper articles appeared, again demonstrating the low opinion that many Americans, and especially Texans, had of Mexico and Mexicans. One paper suggested that what Mexico "most needs is quiet and peace; her masters enlightened and evaluated, her resources developed; her hopes and confidence assured that some form of government should become stable and unchanged."[25] The same paper speculated that Texans were only using Carvajal as a front for Americans to enter Mexico.[26] Mexican officials who read the articles could not comprehend why the United States apparently took no action.

Carvajal persisted in his efforts, appointing a local pro-filibuster newspaper editor as a "general" in his army. In January 1852, Mexican officials advised the United States that Carvajal or members of his party were again crossing the border at various places, sometimes confronting Mexican troops, then withdrawing.[27] On February 20, 1852, Carvajal led 438 men, eighty-four of them Mexicans, back across the Río Bravo. He had one twelve-inch field piece to support his attack. More than 800 Mexican troops under Colonel Valentín Cruz and supported by four cannons met the invaders near Carmargo at 2:00 P.M. on February 21, 1852. A fierce battle raged for three hours as the Texans charged the fortified Mexican positions. Mexican troops fought fiercely, forcing Carvajal to flee north toward the border without his field piece. Carvajal was wounded in the fight and thirty-one Texans and thirteen Mexicans were killed. Texan newspapers announced, however, that the Mexicans had lost more than 200 killed and wounded.[28]

Between March and May of 1852 Carvajal recuperated and reorganized. He again recruited successfully in Texas by playing on the sympathy of anyone who would listen to criticisms of the Mexican government. During May 1852, in Corpus Christi, Texas, he spoke before a large group, which enthusiastically applauded him and his cause. Some Texans, including General

Hugh McLeod—while not joining the expedition—told the crowd that Carvajal was truthful when he spoke of the oppression of the Mexican government. Many in the crowd volunteered immediately.

In mid-June Mexican officials notified the United States that Carvajal was poised on the Río Bravo to lead another expedition into northern Mexico.[29] Several diplomatic dispatches were exchanged between the United States and Mexico; in one of the notes, the Mexicans announced that they had been holding a "lad" named Williams, presumably fifteen or sixteen years old, who had been with Carvajal's expedition in February.[30] General Francisco Avalos ordered the boy's execution late in June or early in July, arousing a storm of ill feelings in the United States toward Mexico.[31] On learning of the boy's death, American officials called it a "murder in cold blood." Mexican officials responded that Williams and three Mexicans from Texas had accompanied Carvajal to Mexico and had been executed for breaking Mexican law. Robert P. Letcher in Mexico advised his government that the attack on Camargo probably had occurred because of Mexican attacks on boats sailing the Río Bravo and that he expected that the boundary between the two countries was "too narrow ever to expect tranquility on the borders."[32]

Meanwhile, Carvajal prepared to enter Mexico again. With 200 men and four artillery pieces he crossed the international line late in August 1852. He remained only until he heard of the approach of Mexican troops, then marched north to seek safety in the United States.[33] In Texas after this foray, he announced that he was expanding his efforts to include Nuevo León.[34] The announcement and the Mexican government's continuing concern prompted more diplomatic exchanges between the two countries, but by this time Letcher had been replaced in Mexico, and on August 10, 1852, Alfred Conkling assumed the position of United States minister plenipotentiary and envoy extraordinary. On April 20, 1853, Antonio López de Santa Anna assumed the presidency of Mexico for the last of his several terms. As the United States hoped to buy what became the Gadsden Purchase area, the secretary of state and ministers in Mexico became more receptive to Mexican concerns about filibustering.

By early April 1853, Carvajal was back in Corpus Christi, seeking more volunteers. But he and several of his lieutenants were finally arrested by United States authorities for violation of neutrality laws.[35] In May, Conkling referred to Carvajal as a "notorious robber" and advised Mexican authorities that the United States would act in good faith to stop his activities.[36] Conkling told Mexican Secretary of Foreign Relations Lucas Alamán, however, that in the United States one accused of a crime had to be confronted with witnesses to the offense or the person would go free.[37] In fact, Carvajal and his men were tried in Galveston in January 1854, and the trial generated considerable newspaper coverage. The trial was a farce. No jury of Texans would convict anyone who wanted to filibuster in Mexico. The men were acquitted on a technicality, but they would not have had anything to fear anyway. Texans did not have a high opinion of Mexicans generally and, during the trial, newspapers in the state referred to the Mexicans as "greasers" who needed the leadership and help of the Texans.[38]

Immediately after his acquittal, Carvajal began recruiting again.[39] Evidently he did not move fast enough for some of his supporters; during August 1854 a group of his recruits attacked Ciudad Victoria without Carvajal's permission. The party included some Mexicans, but most were Texans. They occupied the village until they heard of the approach of 250 Mexican troops under command of Colonel José Barriero. Barriero was marching from Tampico and bringing along two field pieces. The Texans fled north before the Mexicans arrived.[40] In the fall of 1854 several other armed parties made brief forays into Mexico, but there was no large-scale filibustering attempt organized in Texas during the year.[41]

Early in January 1855, rumors again prevailed along the border that Carvajal was organizing another major filibustering effort. It was not until June, however, that he was poised with troops along the Río Bravo. In fact, Carvajal claimed to be greatly encouraged, for it was apparent to him that many Mexicans in the frontier refused to accept federal control from Mexico City. Some local leaders in Nuevo León and other frontier states refused to recognize the central government. Carvajal did not retreat permanently from his goal of controlling northern Mexico. He remained a problem for several years, but ultimately he attempted to legalize his activities in Monterrey, Mexico. Eventually he gained this legitimacy when Benito Juárez appointed him governor of Tamaulipas during the Juárez presidency. In reponse to Mexican criticism of the inability or unwillingness of the United States to stop filibustering, William L. Marcy, secretary of state, offered that the United States would investigate any dereliction of duty on the part of the United States Army, but he suggested that the Mexican internal political problems—which had prompted officials to pull many troops out of the frontier and garrison them near Mexico City—was the most serious problem.[42] Whether this was an accurate statement or not is purely a matter of opinion and speculation. Whatever the reasons the problem seemed endemic to the entire frontier. While Carvajal was creating trouble for Mexico in the northeast, others created difficulty in the far northwest and the United States responded weakly in trying to stop these endeavors, too.

During the early 1850s several enterprising Frenchmen living in San Francisco also believed economic opportunity beckoned south of the border. Although these men were French, they recruited in and left from California. Charles de Pindray reached northern California in 1850, looking for quick riches in the gold fields.[43] Pindray, like so many gold seekers, was unwilling to follow the life of hard work and deprivation of a prospector and soon realized opportunities rested elsewhere. He heard from other Frenchmen and even from a few southerners who were in California that considerable opportunity was available in northern Mexico. He soon decided to lead his own expedition to the south.

Pindray was the son of a reasonably wealthy French businessman, but the younger Pindray was never interested in a business career. He inherited money upon the death of his father, but promptly squandered it on gambling and women. He fled Paris to escape debts, arrived in the United States in 1846, and quickly journeyed to California hoping for easy wealth.[44]

Pindray promptly became disillusioned in California and became a listless drifter working a little on the docks and spending most of his time in San Francisco bars. While there he heard of Mexican colonization opportunities, which he thought might lead to the fortune that had so far eluded him. And, as he soon realized, the Mexican government had authorized some colonization efforts to populate the northern frontier. He learned that the Mexicans were not hostile to Frenchmen, but that his colonization effort could not include Americans.

In 1851 Pindray began to advertise in California newspapers for French colonists, knowing that most of these men also would be eager to exploit any opportunity in Mexico. In truth, Pindray accepted some Americans into his venture, but tried to pass them off as Frenchmen. He received so many inquiries that he was able to charge $40 to $50 to become a member of the group. This provided some immediate financing. Pindray also believed that the Mexican government in the northern states would provide support for the effort. Mexico wanted the frontier settled as quickly as possible to create a buffer zone to protect against Indian raids.[45]

Newspapermen in California speculated that Pindray's expedition was in truth a filibustering venture using Mexican law to enter the country and get a foothold. Many of the eighty-five men who sailed with Pindray aboard the *Cumberland* for Guaymas, Sonora, were Americans, so the assumption was probably accurate. Shortly after Pindray's party arrived at its destination, additional reinforcements joined them, swelling the force to about 150 men.

The voyage to Guaymas had taken about one month because of bad winds and other difficulties. Even so the French party arrived before the Mexicans had expected them, and the Mexican national congress had not yet acted upon a colonizing bill allowing the French to enter the country. President Mariano Arista sent General Miguel Blanco with several hundred troops to watch the French party.[46] Confrontation was avoided when the Mexican congress finally gave Pindray permission to settle. The Sonoran government also cooperated, granting the party approximately three leagues of land near Cocóspera. Pindray soon learned from local Mexican officials just how strong feelings were against Americans, and he told Mexican authorities that he had expelled the *gringos* from his party. In fact, no Americans left.

Pindray and his men established a small colony and then went looking for silver and gold.[47] He wrote back to newspapers in California that Apaches did not have lead for bullets so they made their ammunition out of pure silver. By April, 1852, as a result of Pindray's encouragement of more immigration into northern Mexico from the United States, or because of Pindray's questionable past, the Mexicans decided that the French were not colonists and were in fact a threat to Mexico.

When Pindray's party began only to prospect and to move about in armed parties, the Mexicans decided that they would have to limit the foreigners' activities. The Mexican government refused to give Pindray's party any of the supplies that it had been promised.[48] Pindray then attempted to force the Mexicans to comply by taking a large armed party to Ures, Sonora, to see local authorities. This belligerence, and the fact that some of Pindray's party had strayed too far from their supposed colony, motivated the Mexicans to organize local militia to expel the intruders. En route to Cocóspera from

Ures, Pindray and his men stopped for the night at the small village of Rayón. During the night Pindray died mysteriously. The *Daily Alta California* of August 15, 1852, reported that Pindray "committed suicide by blowing out his brains ... whilst laboring under a high fever, and in a fit of despair." When news of Pindray's death reached his men at Cocóspera, the expedition fell apart. Some hurriedly joined T. P. Sainte-Marie or Count Gaston Raousset-Boulbon, who then were organizing other filibustering expeditions in northern California.[49]

T. P. Sainte-Marie and Pierre Charles de Saint-Amant, the French consular agent at Sacramento, were also interested in the potential of gold and silver mining in northern Sonora. They organized an expedition at Placerville, California, and found easy recruiting from among the many disillusioned French miners in the region. The two led a group of men aboard the brigs *Sonora* and *Hermosillo* to Guaymas. Using Guaymas as a base, they hoped to hunt for mines in the interior of Sonora. The party did discover some evidence of gold and silver, but it was so scattered that it offered little promise. What the Frenchmen did find was a desert, and that there was virtually no way to survive unless they were well equipped. Many of the men died of disease and starvation and the rest suffered enormously. By October the weary survivors had enough of Mexico and made their way slowly out of the country.[50]

Another enterprising Frenchman, who referred to himself as "Count" Gaston Raousset-Boulbon, soon entered Mexico with a large group of filibusters without the pretext of being colonists. Once in Mexico, he grandiously referred to himself as the future "Sultan of Sonora." Raousset was born into a wealthy French family, and like Pindray was a scoundrel as a youth. He, too, inherited family wealth and squandered it foolishly. His inheritance soon disappeared and he set out for the New World, arriving in California on August 22, 1850.[51] He had no wish to labor in mining but did some work for shipping companies in San Francisco. He met Charles de Pindray in a bar, and Pindray offered him a position with his venture. Determined to lead his own filibustering expedition, Raousset declined.[52] Raousset journeyed to Mexico early in 1852 to obtain permission for a "colonization" venture. André Levasseur, French minister in Mexico, tried to intercede on Raousset's behalf, but Mexico refused, despite the offer from a large Franco-Mexican banking house, Jecker, Torre, and Company, to finance part of the venture. Even President Mariano Arista seemed mildly interested.[53]

Although the Mexican government had not given its permission for the venture, Raousset signed a contract with the Jecker, Torre banking house, which established a corporation called La Compañía Restaurada de la Mina de la Arizona. According to the agreement, Raousset was supposed to recruit 150 Frenchmen in San Francisco. To this point the endeavor appeared a legitimate colonization effort waiting for Mexican sanction.

Raousset returned to San Francisco in April 1852 to organize. He promised that there would be ample opportunity in the mines for anyone interested in working. While he was recruiting in California, another banking firm, the Barron, Forbes, and Company, tried to take over the mining and colonization idea, and created problems with the Mexican government by its lobbying.[54] Raousset found recruiting easy in San Francisco, even though he followed Mexican law and attempted to exclude Americans from his initial effort. He quickly recruited more than 200 men and divided them into military companies each with a commander. Preparations made, the group boarded the *Archibald Gracie* and prepared to sail. Before they got underway, customs officials inspected the ship and asked for verification that the party was a legal colonizing venture.[55] Newspapers in California had carried the details of this expedition for weeks and pronounced it a filibuster. Raousset, however, convinced the officials of his cooperation with Mexican authorities. The ship was allowed to leave early on May 24, 1852. Mexican authorities, however, did not cooperate. In fact, Mexican consular agents and other officials kept the Mexican government informed of the movements of all potential filibustering groups. In August 1852 the Mexicans heard that 2000 filibusters were headed for Sonora and would be reinforced by approximately 6000 additional men.[56]

The *Archibald Gracie* and its well-armed contingent arrived at Guaymas, Sonora, where local citizens greeted the men warmly. Raousset learned, however, that official Mexican attitudes were greatly different; both state and national authorities were openly hostile. Mexican troops under command of General Miguel Blanco ordered the Frenchmen to stop in Guaymas and not to head inland. Blanco told Raousset to lead his party west of Guaymas to Pozo and remain there until told differently.[57] The Frenchman realized that something was amiss, but assumed that going to Pozo as ordered was the best temporary move. Raousset led his men to the specified site and waited for word from Blanco. When no information came from the Mexican military commander, Raousset led his men to Ures, Sonora, where he hoped to talk with state officials.[58]

The Frenchmen were well armed, including having two field pieces. André Levasseur in Mexico City heard of the problems between Raousset and the local authorities and decided to withdraw from any participation in the venture. Meanwhile, Raousset and his men arrived at Ures and the French leader talked with the governor of Sonora. No agreement could be reached between the governor and Raousset at this time. The governor advised Raousset to return to Guaymas where some of the French troops left behind were causing difficulties. Raousset retraced his steps to Guaymas. General Blanco told him he should lead his men inland to Hermosillo and Raousset complied. Once at Hermosillo, he received another note from Blanco telling him to leave his men and proceed with a small detachment to Arizpe to negotiate. Raousset ignored the request. Instead he wrote a note to friends in San Francisco that—though prospects looked bleak—he expected all to work out in his favor.[59]

On July 27, 1852, Raousset led his party out of Hermosillo in full military dress. Mexican authorities warned him not to make such a display. And, again General Blanco ordered the French leader to come to Arizpe to talk. On one occasion Raousset started north, but met survivors of the Pindray expedition, who undoubtedly told him of their misfortune. Raousset immediately rejoined his men.[60] Blanco was furious that his orders were again ignored, and he ordered troops from across the state to join him in a campaign against the Frenchmen. In October the Sonoran congress abrogated all earlier agreements with the French colonists and appropriated money to finance a military campaign against them. Raousset, however, had already announced to local Mexicans that he intended to become the "Sultan of Sonora."[61] Blanco attempted on several occasions to resolve the matter peacefully, telling Raousset that he would issue letters of security for the Frenchmen to leave Mexico if they would put down their arms.

Surely having heard stories of the problems of the Pindray expedition, the intruders voted to fight. Raousset decided to occupy Hermosillo and make his stand there. Blanco heard of Raousset's intentions and hurried to Hermosillo to fortify the position. Blanco had only 240 men and a few volunteers. Raousset was aware that his group would have superiority in arms and trained men. Raousset's party attacked Hermosillo and within two hours

Guaymas, Sonora *(courtesy of Arizona Historical Society, Tucson, #78509).*

Hermosillo, Sonora *(courtesy of Arizona Historical Society, Tucson, #43053).*

captured the city, suffering eighteen killed and thirty-two wounded. Mexican losses were twenty killed and more than fifty wounded.[62]

For the moment, Raousset was in control of Hermosillo; the Sonorans, however, organized to throw him out of the country. But fate entered the plan. Raousset had lost three of his best lieutenants in the fighting at Hermosillo, and now he and many of his men and surviving lieutenants contracted severe dysentery. Lack of medical attention and other hardships prompted him to ask the Mexicans to allow them to go to Guaymas where they could take passage by sea to the United States. Manuel María Gandara, governor at the time, agreed, but did not so advise General Blanco. Blanco heard of the French movement and hastened to Guaymas with a force of about 500 men determined to fight.[63] By this time Raousset was so weak that he could not walk. He asked for terms. On November 4, 1852, Blanco accepted the surrender of the entire French party. Most of the survivors made their way either by ship or overland back to California.

Mazatlan, Sinoloa *(courtesy of Arizona Historical Society, Tucson, #25-14544-5).*

Raousset remained in Mazatlán until early 1853, recovering from his illness. He was, however, determined to lead another filibustering expedition as soon as he recuperated.[64] Once again the activities of this adventurer added to the confusion created by other filibusters trying to organize expeditions. On May 19, 1853, just a little over two weeks after considerable discussion had taken place over Carvajal's early violation of Mexican territory, Alfred Conkling in Mexico City advised Secretary of State William Marcy that the trouble in which Raousset found himself was the result of "shameful duplicity and the most revolting perfidy."[65] In view of Conkling's comments to the Mexican authorities and to Marcy, it did not appear that he was candid in his communications to the Mexicans. The Mexican secretary of foreign relations did not believe the United States was sincere in its actions. He told Conkling that the Raousset expedition had been organized "with the knowledge and permission of the authorities without any attempt on the part of the latter to prevent it as they might easily have done."[66] Raousset arrived back in California in January 1853.[67] Before long, he received a letter from André Levasseur, French ambassador in Mexico, inviting him to talk with Mexican President Antonio López de Santa Anna. Raousset wanted to do some recruiting for a new venture before he left for Mexico, and he did not arrive until July 7, 1853. He intended to pressure the Mexican president into naming him governor of Sonora.[68] For four months Raousset remained in Mexico City, trying in vain to get Santa Anna to agree to his scheme. The wily Mexican dictator, in deep trouble with political enemies, would have nothing to do with the adventuresome Frenchman. In fact, Santa Anna even advised Levasseur that he opposed Raousset bringing honest settlers or anyone else to Sonora.

Manuel María Gandara, still governor in Sonora, watched the events in Mexico City carefully, and he prepared to resist any French intrusion, government sanctioned or not. Despite public opposition to Raousset's plan, the Santa Anna regime hinted that it might grant Raousset permission to bring 500 colonists to the frontier if he met certain conditions. Raousset would not discuss any terms except his own, and the negotiations ended. Raousset returned to California and announced that he would lead a military expedition into Mexico.[69]

By this time, Mexicans were disgusted with French and American filibustering expeditions, but Mexican newspapers early in 1854 continued to print stories of the impending return of the "Sultan of Sonora."[70] Mexico would be prepared if Raousset and his filibusters arrived. Santa Anna appointed José María Yáñez military governor of Sonora with orders to expel intruders. Yáñez prepared to resist *filibusteros*, and Santa Anna issued a proclamation against filibustering. To discourage filibustering in large parties, Santa Anna offered to take foreigners into the Mexican army on the frontier, and to give them the opportunity to own land. He hoped to strip Raousset of support by giving Raousset's men an opportunity if they wanted to work for it.[71]

In at least one instance, some 400 Frenchmen on board a British registered ship, the *Challenge*, sailed for Guaymas ostensibly to accept the Mexican offer. Raousset and his associates were aware of the effort to thwart their expedition and had infiltrated the group, but Raousset was unable to accompany the men to Mexico. General John E. Wool and United States Army troops were watching his activities too closely. The 400 men sailed for Guaymas on April 1, 1854, with Raousset's lieutenants in control.[72]

Raousset remained in San Francisco gathering supplies and more recruits. He planned to join the advance party once it had reached Guaymas. José María Yáñez also prepared for Raousset's arrival. Yañez, long in Mexican army service, arrived at Ures, Sonora, on April 18,1854.[73] Two days later he learned of the landing of Raousset's men at Guaymas on the *Challenge*. Yáñez quickly journeyed to the port. He knew that some of the men came as a legitimate group according to Santa Anna's agreement, but he did not wish to allow the party freedom of movement or many firearms until he was certain he could take control.

Between May 23 and 25, 1854, Raousset and a few of his closest associates left San Francisco bound for Guaymas on board the *Belle*. They carried 180 rifles and ammunition for many other types of weapons. He left a letter for Patrice Dillon, the French consul in San Francisco, telling him of the duplicity of the Mexicans and the need for Raousset to join his men and force the Mexicans to stand by the legal agreements Santa Anna had promised. Dillon was probably involved all along, but he insisted that Raousset give him a letter that kept the French official at a distance from the scheme.[74]

Raousset's voyage was extremely rough, and ultimately the boat capsized near Magdalena Bay but the water was shallow enough to allow the men to save most of the cargo. Eventually, Raousset and party, replete with most of the supplies, reached Guaymas. Yáñez had captured two of Raousset's men earlier and learned of Raousset's impending arrival.[75] On July 3, 1854, Raousset entered Guaymas in disguise and joined his men. Soon all the faithful party had taken up positions near the bay. Raousset planned his next move. Meanwhile, Yáñez rallied his troops and volunteers and encircled the French position. On July 13, the Mexican general tried to convince the Frenchmen to surrender without bloodshed. Raousset would have none of it. He was convinced that a few shots would send the Mexicans fleeing for safety. He had sorely underestimated Yáñez and his men.[76] Raousset ordered his force to establish positions where they could fire on the defenders, then use their bayonets to charge the Mexican position. A fierce battle ensued from 2:00 P.M. until after 5:00 on July 13. At the first Mexican barrage, more than a half of the Frenchmen fled to the American consul's house for protection. With the bay at their backs and Mexicans in front of them, the survivors put up a strong fight but could not escape. The entire French party surrendered after forty-eight of their number had been killed and seventy-eight wounded. The Mexicans captured 313 *filibusteros* in the fight; the Mexicans suffered nineteen killed and forty-five wounded.[77] Mexican authorities deported most of the Frenchmen, but they conducted a military court martial of Raousset. They found him guilty of violating Mexican laws and placed him in front of a firing squad on August 12, 1854, hoping to send notice to all would-be filibusters that Mexico would not allow intervention under any conditions.

While Raousset's venture was in the process of failing, yet another dreamer was scheming to lead a group of Americans south.[78] William Walker, "the grey eyed man of destiny," as he was later described, was born in Tennessee and was lured to California during the gold rush. He arrived in San Francisco in 1850 and worked as a newspaper editor for a time. He was trained as a medical doctor and had read law. He practiced law briefly in California.[79] In fact, Walker and his law partner, Henry P. Watkins, read about the exploits of Raousset-Boulbon and decided that leading a group into Mexico was a good idea. Californians agreed and some even offered to contribute money to the scheme. Walker also had heard of Raousset's fate and of Mexican hostility toward such ventures. That did not deter him or his partner. In May 1853 the two traveled to Guaymas to see just what the Mexican attitude toward "colonizers" was after the Raousset affair. Although they did not talk to Governor Manuel María Gandara, they decided that there was considerable opportunity south of the border.[80]

Walker and Watkins returned to California and immediately began recruiting for a filibustering expedition. When newspapers carried stories of Walker's efforts, the Mexican government again quickly learned of his plans. Mexican Secretary of Foreign Relations Manuel Díaz de Bonilla protested to James Gadsden, United States minister in Mexico. The Mexicans were certain that Sonora was Walker's target, but they were correct only in part. Actually Walker planned to create the Republic of Sonora with Baja California as a state.[81] Recruiting men for filibustering expeditions to Mexico remained easy. Walker had many more volunteers than he could control. He began selling bonds to finance his new republic, raising considerable money. San Francisco newspapers carried his advertisements for the bonds, causing tense correspondence between the United States and Mexico. By the end of September 1853, Walker had completed his preparations, including the acquisition of a bark, the *Arrow*, on which his initial party would sail.

This time the United States did not ignore the filibustering, and the army dispatched General Ethan A. Hitchcock to California with orders to prevent such illegal *entradas*. Hitchcock seized Walker's ship briefly, but found no evidence that the bark was outfitted for a filibustering expedition, although it contained some camping equipment and boxes of ammunition. None of this appeared to Hitchcock as sufficient evidence of a filibustering expedition. The day after the seizure, the army turned the bark over to the United States marshal. Shortly, the local district attorney responded to popular pressure and returned the boat to Walker and his associates. According to Californians, anyone rumored to be planning a filibustering expedition from California to Mexico was a hero.[82]

Walker was not present to collect his ship, however. He and forty-five heavily armed men had sailed for Mexico on the bark *Caroline*, a vessel licensed in Mexico and owned by the son of the U.S. consul at Guaymas. Other men would join later. Walker and his party put in at Cabo San Lucas for supplies, and waited for reinforcements that Henry Watkins was bringing from California. Watkins failed to arrive, so Walker and his group set out again.[83] On November 3, 1853, the enthusiastic filibusters sailed into the harbor at La Paz, Baja California. They took control of the village and arrested Mexican Governor Colonel Rafael Espinosa. Within thirty minutes

Walker had captured the entire village, lowered the Mexican flag, and proclaimed the establishment of the Republic of Lower California.[84] It soon became evident to Walker and his men, however, that they could neither hold the area with so few men nor could they invade Sonora. They contented themselves with plundering the town for three days and left on November 6.

Walker's activities in Baja California corresponded with the period when the United States was negotiating with Mexico for the purchase of the Mesilla Strip. The Mexicans demanded that the United States send a warship to Baja California to keep Walker from moving inland and to help protect the Mexican coastline from the pirates.[85] Even if the U.S. agreed to the request, it had no ship in position to take action. Mexican authorities reinforced their troops at Guaymas and waited for Walker. It was then that the defenders learned that Walker had occupied La Paz.[86]

In Baja California, Walker adopted the Civil Code of Louisiana, which legalized slavery in his new republic.[87] While Walker was still in La Paz, local citizens organized an armed rebellion that prompted the "Battle of La Paz," after which Walker claimed he reestablished control before departing. Seven Mexicans were killed in the fight.[88]

Walker and party then sailed again to Cabo San Lucas, a small indefensible town far to the south where they arrived on November 8. A Mexican warship appeared on the horizon, causing Walker to reevaluate his position. He sailed to Ensenada (Bahía) de Todos Santos, where he believed he could establish a base close enough to the United States. The adventurer remained at Ensenada and sent his Secretary of State Frederick Emory to California to gather supplies and recruit more men. When Emory arrived in California, newspapers there hailed Walker's efforts as "another advance toward that manifest destiny of the Anglo Saxon race." Californians treated Emory as a hero. One editor wrote that his arrival "excited our American population to the wildest bounds of joy."[89] Emory opened a recruiting office in San Francisco and unfurled the flag of the Republic of Lower California over the door.

Walker, who had sailed to Ensenada on the *Caroline* holding a Mexican official captured at La Paz, left the ship's captain on board with a few crewmen and the captured Mexican and went into Ensenada. While Walker was planning his next move, the ship's captain—who had been convinced by the hostage of the danger he was in by helping Walker—sailed away, stranding Walker and his party. Walker's problems were multiplied by his loss of the ship and most of his supplies. Moreover, Mexicans in Ensenada had fought hard to keep him out of the village, and they remained a problem after Walker captured the town. In mid-December the Mexicans laid siege to Ensenada in an attempt to oust the intruders.[90] Walker recognized his vulnerability, but he ordered some of his men to follow him in an attack on Santo Tomás, a military colony about thirty miles south of Ensenada. Walker's bid to reach the post was repulsed by the defenders, who halted his attack after a vicious exchange of gunfire. Walker led his men back to Ensenada and welcomed 200 reinforcements who arrived on the *Anita*. Unfortunately, the replacements brought almost no supplies; food was especially short.[91]

Near Guaymas more than 2000 Mexican soldiers organized to march to Baja California to deal with Walker. Despite Walker's precarious position, on January 18, 1854, he announced from Ensenada that he was changing the name of his country to the Republic of Sonora, with Baja California and Sonora as the two states. During the last days of January, he learned that a Mexican warship, accompanied by the *U.S.S. Portsmouth*, a ship the United States Navy had assigned to the region, was approaching Ensenada.[92] By early February, Walker recognized that he was in trouble. The Mexican ship and its escort were standing off shore, presumably awaiting the arrival of Mexican troops. On February 13, Walker led a party of 130 men northward, promising his followers that they were going to Sonora. Walker's party had already dwindled to less than one-third its original size as a result of desertion, and during this march more men decided to abandon the effort. In fact, his force evaporated so quickly that he had to reconsider his plans.[93]

Events were not going well in California either. Frederick Emory, recruiting in San Diego, had been arrested and charged with complicity in a filibustering scheme. The United States Army, under new commander General John E. Wool, also took steps to stop filibustering. Early in February Wool learned that Walker and his party had left Ensenada, destination unknown.[94] Walker, in fact, had led his men north to the small village of San Vicente, where he faced additional hostility. On March 20, after resting near San Vicente, he led his men north to the mouth of the Colorado River. By early April he was camped near the river and he made forays into Sonora.

When he entered Sonora, Mexicans fought him with whatever arms they could gather. Local resistance in Sonora was led by Guadalupe Meléndrez, whom Walker referred to as a bandit.[95]

On May 1, 1854, after heavy skirmishing with Mexicans, Walker and his band, now numbering about fifty men, retraced their steps to Ensenada. Facing increasing resistance, the filibusters left for San Diego. On May 8, the Americans got to the border where they found Meléndrez and a sizeable Mexican force blocking their escape to the U.S. Walker decided that the only way to safety was to charge directly into Meléndrez and his men. Seeing the Americans running at them, shooting and shouting, the Mexicans retreated, allowing Walker and his survivors to escape.[96]

While the drama between the Mexicans and Walker's men occurred at the border, a United States Army detachment and several dozen citizens from San Diego—who had heard of Walker's plight—watched from a nearby hill as the filibuster was taken into custody by American authorities. He was brought to trial in San Diego for filibustering, but quickly acquitted by a friendly jury of Californians. He went on in a couple of years to filibuster in Nicaragua.

4

1855-1860

During the summer and fall of 1855, Juan (Jean) Napoleón Zerman planned and led an expedition from San Francisco to Baja California. Zerman, like other adventurers before and after him, sought fame and fortune south of the border. Zerman claimed he led an expedition into Mexico at the invitation of Juan Alvarez and Ignacio Comonfort, who under the *Plan de Ayutla* were trying to overthrow Antonio López de Santa Anna. From the beginning, Zerman insisted he was not a filibuster.[1]

Zerman was born of Alsatian or Corsican parents in Venice, Italy, in 1795. He was educated at the Naval School of Venicia and was fascinated with military life and yearned for a military career. During his youth he lived in London, Greece, and France. In 1826 he claimed his French citizenship (his father had been a French military officer in Italy) and joined the French army as a lieutenant. In 1831 Louis-Philippe, King of France (1830-1848), sent the eager young Zerman to Italy to foment a revolution to unite Italy and France. Probably through his own carelessness—if later events were any indication of his character—his scheme was discovered and Zerman was arrested. He was held for eight years before the French were able to win his release. Zerman returned to France in 1839 anxious to serve Louis-Philippe, who accepted his enthusiastic devotion. In 1840 the king sent him on yet another mission—this time to Spain to carry out various intrigues with members of the Spanish government. Whatever his assignment, he accomplished little; the next year he was sent to Egypt and Syria on new assignments. Zerman was on this mission when the French king was deposed. Zerman returned to France and cast about for new ventures.[2]

Zerman made his first of several trips to the United States in the 1840s. He marched with General Winfield Scott to Mexico City during the war with Mexico. Attracted to the California gold fields and promise of easy wealth, he decided to move west in 1850. He arrived early in the year and looked for easy-money opportunities. He did not have the patience or dedication to hard work that would allow him to succeed, but he briefly tried commerce in San Francisco. In this foray into the world of business he probably met Roark (Roderick) Matheson, a successful entrepreneur in the fledgling city. Matheson had a vision of opening up new markets in Baja California, even of acquiring considerable land if the opportunity arose. Matheson claimed he was in contact with General Juan Alvarez and had volunteered to help the Mexicans fighting Santa Anna raise money for arms and ammunition if Alvarez would guarantee to him land in the state of Guerrero. Alvarez asked Matheson to help him raise 100,000 pesos to purchase needed supplies, but he would not grant land rights. According to Matheson, Alvarez offered to pay twelve percent interest on the money and promised that the state of Guerrero would begin repaying the money one year after Santa Anna's ouster.[3]

Zerman claimed that he had communicated directly with Alvarez in the early summer of 1855, telling Alvarez that he would raise a contingent of men and secure a sufficient number of ships to blockade all the Pacific coast ports still under Santa Anna's control. Zerman later insisted that Alvarez told him in August that he was interested in helping to supply troops struggling against Santa Anna's supporters in the interior of the country but that additional men would not be needed. Alvarez told Zerman that he had already made arrangements with Matheson to raise money to help his troops. Zerman was not discouraged. He went immediately to talk to Matheson. Exactly what occurred in the conversations is unknown. Zerman evidently explained his scheme to an eager Matheson. Matheson told him he was raising money for Alvarez and was also interested in Zerman's plan. Zerman responded that once in Mexico with his men he would organize and appoint officials for his government. He hoped to become a permanent official after the mission was completed.[4]

Matheson had access to the brig *Archibald Gracie*, whose captain and eighty-five adventurers had planned originally to join William Walker, then in Nicaragua. The captain and the men were intrigued with the idea of blockading Mexican ports and eventually getting important roles in the new government in Baja California. Matheson's only problem had been finding someone to lead the expedition. Zerman solved that problem by volunteering to work with Matheson and his partners. Zerman also claimed to have access to more men in San Francisco and said he could provide another brig carrying an arms cache of six canon, eighty carbines, and forty pistols. On October 11, 1855, after striking a deal with Matheson, Zerman boarded the *Archbibald Gracie* with his wife and two children, personal possessions and official entourage; they left San Francisco heading south. He carried several official-looking documents from Matheson and a letter from Alvarez saying additional financial help was needed. The documents showed that Matheson and his partners had authorized the venture and that Zerman would be Matheson's agent in Mexico. Zerman was to sail to La Paz, capital of Baja California, and establish a provisional government in preparation for blockading the west coast of the Mexican mainland. He would be an admiral in the Mexican navy, receiving 600 pesos monthly salary and an additional 400 monthly for expenses. After sailing eight days, the party arrived at Cabo San Lucas, where Zerman sighted the brig *Rebecca Adams* under command of Captain Thomas Andrews.[5] Zerman promised Andrews 500 pesos monthly plus pay for his crew for ninety days if Andrews would help. Afterward Mexico would pay Andrews and his crew. Andrews did not know what to think of Zerman, but after noting the Mexican flag Zerman's boat was flying and the Mexican-style naval uniforms, he decided that Zerman was indeed whom he claimed to be. Zerman even showed him a letter that he said was from Juan Alvarez; the document convinced the skeptical captain that he was dealing with a legitimate Mexican agent and agreed to assist in whatever way possible.

The two ships gathered what supplies they could find and sailed for La Paz. Near Cabo San Lucas the party encountered the Mexican brig *Cavitera*. Zerman told her captain that he was commandeering the ship and crew to join the expedition. The Mexican captain thought he had no choice but to abide by the orders of the so-called admiral. By this time Zerman learned of the fall of Santa Anna and with his tiny armada headed directly to La Paz.

Meanwhile, General don José María Blancarte, comandante principal and jefe político of Baja California, learned of Zerman's approach. He quickly broadcast that American *filibusteros* were en route and he needed all troops and volunteers to come to La Paz at once. National militia and *vecinos* arrived to fortify the city. They mounted cannons aimed at the entrance to the port and prepared for a fight. On November 13, 1855, Zerman's "fleet" appeared off the port entrance. Zerman sailed up a short canal, pausing to send word that he had arrived to take over. He sent a note to Blancarte explaining that he was an agent of General Juan Alvarez and was authorized to blockade the port. Included in the message were copies of Zerman's documents replete with the signatures of his newly appointed government officials. He advised Blancarte that he, Zerman, held the rank of admiral of the Mexican Navy, and that once in control he guaranteed to all citizens their rights. He would establish a free trade zone in the city. He told Blancarte he wanted to talk for thirty minutes directly with him.

Blancarte was not amused, frightened, or impressed with the display of papers and the grandiose language. He advised Zerman to stay on board his ship and not to disembark, telling him that he considered the party an illegal filibuster and that Mexican law called for all *filibusteros* to be shot. He intended to carry out the law if Zerman did not leave at once.[6] Zerman foolishly ignored Blancarte's warning. With a small party, including his young son and so-called government officials, he boarded a skiff and headed for shore. The only Mexican with the Zerman party, Fernando (or Francisco) Palacios, Zerman's secretary, went along as translator. Zerman was attired in a uniform of his own design. The strange and gaudy looking piece was a combination of the Mexican and English naval officer's formal dress. The oddest part was a sombrero from which two chicken feathers protruded.

On reaching shore Zerman and his party were taken prisoner by Manuel Márquez, captain of the local *guardia nacional,* and escorted to see Blancarte. The Mexican general was not impressed with the uniform or with Zerman and dryly informed him that he was under arrest and would be tried as a filibuster. Zerman protested vigorously, but the objections fell on deaf ears; Blancarte was well aware of the continuing efforts of Americans to interfere with local Mexican matters. Shortly afterward Blancarte ordered the men on the boats to surrender. They refused at first, but the vessels had sailed into a narrow canal and had no room to run or manuever. All Blancarte had to do was station his cannon in strategic locations and fire a salvo to convince the filibusters to surrender. One man was killed and two wounded in the salvo. Zerman's men quickly hoisted a white flag and obediently disembarked. The comic-opera of Zerman parading ashore in a silly uniform ended his threat as a filibuster. It did not, however, end the affair for Zerman or for the

United States government. Blancarte sent Zerman and his party to the mainland and ultimately to Mexico City. All the while Zerman demanded his
rights. He wanted to see Alvarez. Blancarte had confiscated his ships and
supplies and Zerman wanted Alvarez to set things straight and return his
possessions. Alvarez, however, kept his distance. He was aware that any
involvement with an American filibuster would spell political suicide for him
or any other Mexican who had dealings with the intruders. There followed
a long series of events in which Zerman unsuccessfully tried to see Alvarez.
Zerman was eventually released, but he continued to try to recover his property and to exonerate himself of all charges.

The United States government was more concerned about the fate of
Thomas Andrews than that of Zerman. Authorities said Zerman had been
dishonest with Andrews. They also told the Mexicans that Blancarte had not
been honest in describing the sequence of events at La Paz; they claimed, in
fact, that Blancarte had invited Zerman to have dinner with him, then
arrested him. Moreover, Blancarte had fired upon the Zerman party before
offering an explanation of opposition to the party and had treated his prisoners as criminals. He even confiscated the men's personal possessions. The
prisoners ultimately had been marched to Mexico City and later claimed
that the Mexican soldiers abused them.[7]

Zerman insisted that he was not a filibuster and in his mind he may not
have been, but most Mexicans considered him as such and that point was
significant to United States-Mexican relations. Again, it appeared to
Mexicans that the United States did not care whether armed parties entered
Mexico from north of the border and, in fact, probably supported the
efforts. Ultimately, Zerman made his way back to California. He did not
receive compensation from the Mexican government for his losses, though
the Mexicans did later return some possessions. On November 25, 1857, the
Mexican supreme court decided that Zerman may not have been a filibuster;
after deliberation the court ordered reimbursement for the confiscation of
the *Rebecca Adams* and damages for its crew. Zerman received no damages,
nor did the Mexican government pay for the confiscated *Archibald Gracie*.
The stage was set for a violent confrontation should someone else attempt to
enter Mexico with hostile intentions.[8]

In the late summer of 1856, John Forsyth became the new United States
minister to Mexico. Filibustering in the form of the Napoleón Zerman and

Henry A. Crabb expeditions had either just entered Mexico or were planning to do so. Forsyth believed that "this unhappy country is again on the
verge of political revolution."[9] In fact, he believed that Mexicans desired
United States intervention. He expressed that attitude when he advised
William Marcy that "I am every day made sensible of a prevalent and growing sentiment among intelligent Mexicans, that without the intervention,
and, or guarantees of the United States, in some form or other, a stable government can never be secured to this people." He advised that Americans
should seek control of church power in Mexico, integrate themselves into
the Mexican Army, and take action to protect Americans and their property
in Mexico. How such acts could be accomplished and why the Catholic
Church was part of the statement is unclear. Americans, according to
Forsyth, should also neogotiate a liberal trade treaty and eventually create an
American protectorate.[10] The minister claimed that the Zerman expedition
was indeed working with Juan Alvarez's revolutionaries and that Zerman had
arrived in Mexico "to find the friends whom they had come to succor, in
power and their services not needed." When Zerman arrived off the coast of
Mexico, the general in charge of the region began a "cruel and barbarous
sequel of acts which must forever disgrace that person as a Christian man, a
gentleman and a magistrate. Zerman and a number of officers were enticed
on shore by a treacherous invitation to dine with 'His Excellency General
Blancarte.' Instead of hospitality, the guests met with bayonets and chains."
The ships were then "plundered" and one American was killed.[11] The
Mexican government responded to Forsyth's comments, saying that this was
an internal affair and the United States had no part in its solution. Forsyth
angrily reponded that he found the Mexican government's note "objection-
able," and that General Blancarte's treatment of Zerman was "barbarous and
grossly violated the usages of civilized nations." Forsyth then sent a nineteen-
page letter to Antonio de la Fuente detailing the Zerman expedition and
stating that Zerman had been enticed to enter Mexico by the Alvarez faction.[12] Miguel Lerdo de Tejada, secretary of development, responded a
month later, telling Forsyth that Zerman's expedition "exhibits the charac-
teristics of a 'marauding and filibuster' got up against the peace, the dignity
and the territory of the Mexican Republic, violating the neutrality laws of
the United States and unlawfully changing its flag on the high seas."[13]

In 1857 the Mexican frontier remained exposed to attacks by hostile

Indians and an endless number of filibusters who dreamed of making easy fortunes. One such adventurer who saw opportunity in northwestern Mexico was Henry Alexander Crabb, a former state senator in California. Bearded and dark-eyed, Crabb was born in Tennessee where he learned the fundamentals necessary to become a lawyer. With news of the gold discoveries in California, Crabb was eager to make his fortune in the far West. Early in 1849 he traveled to California, where he soon became involved in politics.[14]

Shortly after arriving in California, Crabb met and married the daughter of the prominent California-Sonora Ainsa family. His marriage into so prestigious a family provided him political connections in Sonora. Crabb was keenly interested in Mexico and he knew that the liberal and conservative forces in Sonora were struggling for control of the state. Don Ignacio Pesqueira and don Manuel María Gandara were the leaders of the two factions and both wanted to be governor.[15] In June 1855, Crabb said that he and his brother-in-law Augustín Ainsa traveled to Sonora by ship and talked with influential businessmen. Crabb claimed that the same men who supported Pesqueira suggested to him that he might aid their cause and help control Indians by bringing a group of Americans to the state to colonize the frontier. The visit set off a considerable amount of speculation about the involvement of local Mexicans in the "colonization" effort that Crabb was planning.[16]

During the summer of 1856, while Crabb was back in California attempting to establish his venture, full scale fighting broke out between the two Sonoran factions. Supporters of Manuel María Gandara accused Pesqueira of encouraging Crabb to bring Americans to the state. The Gandara partisans hoped that this would cast Pesqueira in a bad light and cause him to lose the support of local citizens who hated any *gringo* intrusion or anyone who cooperated with the Americans. Although the Gandarist faction made its charges against Pesqueira widely known, Pesqueira managed to get control of the state before Crabb and his party got underway.[17] Crabb was aware of the changes in political fortunes in Sonora, but he continued to organize the Arizona Colonization Company. Many members of the company of about 1000 were wealthy and influential Californians. In January 1857, Crabb and some of his recruits sailed to Los Angeles, where they assembled supplies and added more excited members. They marched to present-day Yuma, Arizona, and after a short stay moved south into Sonora.[18]

Crabb's party traveled slowly because of the extreme desert conditions.

Crabb kept the press of California informed of his progress and the papers carried reports on the expedition. John Forsyth, U.S. minister to Mexico, advised the U.S. government that Mexico City newspapers had been carrying rumors of Crabb's expedition for weeks. Forsyth was fearful that the Mexicans would not be easy on another filibustering expedition. As early as February 20, 1857, in fact, the Mexican government was already well informed of Crabb's plans.[19]

Crabb's party, about ninety men, headed southeast along the Gila River. They crossed the border near Sonoita where Crabb wrote a message on March 26, 1857, to José María Redondo, prefect of Altar, telling him that the Crabb venture was a legal colonizing effort and that they were en route to the interior of Mexico.[20] Redondo did not respond, but Pesqueira did, advising Crabb through a proclamation to the people of Sonora that he would not tolerate *filibusteros*. In the same notice, Pesqueira called on all Sonorans to let their "conciliation become sincere in order to fight this horde of pirates, without country, religion, or honor." Crabb clearly was not welcome in Mexico.[21] The *gringo* ignored all warnings and led his party toward the Mexican village of Caborca. He took sixty-nine men some ninety miles south, leaving twenty others to follow later. The Mexicans were not idle in their preparations. In Guaymas, General Luis Noriega, commandante of the local garrison, called on his men to march toward Crabb's party, urging them to show no mercy for the "rascals."[22]

Mexicans in Caborca learned of Crabb's band before it arrived on April 1, 1857. As Crabb's men walked in disorderly fashion through a wheat field toward the village, the Mexicans opened fire with rifles and pistols. Crabb's group was taken by surprise, but they acquitted themselves well, killing several defenders. Fighting ceased for a short while and then the Americans fought their way across the clearing to the village. The defenders withdrew to the church in the town plaza, where they hoped to fend off the Americans.[23] Five Americans had been killed and fifteen wounded in the house-to-house fighting. Mexicans suffered even higher casualties but they refused to surrender. Crabb then attempted to get into the church where the Mexicans had taken a defensive position, sending fifteen men with a keg of dynamite to try to blow down the heavy wooden door of the building. The Mexicans mounted a fierce barrage of rifle fire that took the lives of five more of Crabb's command. Although the dynamite exploded, it was not close enough to the door to do major damage.[24]

Caborca in the distance as Crabb's men might have seen as they advanced toward the village. Below, La Purísima Concepción de Caborca *(both photos courtesy of Arizona Historical Society, Tucson, #s 16259 and 48401).*

For six days the two groups held their positions. Unfortunately for Crabb more Mexican troops and armed volunteers arrived to surround the buildings where the Americans had established their stronghold. By April 6 more than 1500 defenders with a large number of Papago Indian allies had the Crabb party under siege. On that day one of the Indians fired a flaming arrow into the thatched roof of the filibuster's stronghold and the conflagration threatened the entire party. To remove the burning roof, Crabb ordered all the men to one end of the building and he placed a keg of dynamite at the other. He then proceeded to attempt to blow off the roof of the building. He was partially successful, but several of his men were wounded in the explosion.

Realizing that he was badly outnumbered, Crabb asked Hilario Gabilondo, the Mexican military commander, for terms of surrender. Gabilondo told him he and his men would be treated as prisoners of war and given medical attention and food. Although some of his men wanted to fight, Crabb decided to surrender. The filibusters soon learned that they had made a grave, fatal mistake. Gabilondo had no intention of following any rules of war. The men were not given medical attention nor food and water; instead they were herded into a corral at the edge of town where they were held for the night. The next morning they were marched to the outskirts of the village and shot down in groups of five. Mexicans were heard to boast, according to the only survivor— a sixteen-year-old American boy —that their hogs were feeding on the bodies of "Los Yankees." Crabb suffered a solitary death in the town plaza. He was given his last rites and placed before a firing squad. Afterward, a soldier severed Crabb's head with his sabre and placed it in a jar of mescal for preservation.[25]

Gabilondo's men searched the surrounding country to make sure they had gotten all filibusters. At Dunbar's store just across the border in the United States they found four men who had been too ill to go with Crabb. The Mexicans captured and executed them. Finally, the Mexicans encountered another party of Crabb's filibusters who had organized into the Tucson Valley Company. Under the command of Major R. N. Wood and Captain Granville H. Oury, they were about fifteen miles north of Caborca when the Mexicans intercepted them. Captain José Moreno of Altar told the *gringos* that if they surrendered they would be treated as prisoners. Although they knew nothing of Crabb's fate, they decided on battle. After attacking vigorously, they used the confusion to flee toward the United States. Sixteen more members of the Crabb party were not so fortunate. Confronted by the same group of Mexican soldiers who had been at Dunbar's store, the Americans surrendered and were shot.[26]

On May 30, 1857, John Forsyth advised don Juan Antonio de la Fuente, secretary of foreign relations, that the execution of Crabb and his party was "unmitigated murder." Crabb and his men, Forsyth claimed, were innocent immigrants with family ties in Mexico.[27] The Mexican government responded that Crabb's party had entered Mexico as an armed group without permission and that it was a filibustering expedition. In accordance with Mexican law concerning such intrusion, the invaders had been executed. Mexico offered no apologies. When authorities in California advised the government that they believed Crabb had broken Mexican law, the United States dropped the matter.[28] In dealing violently with the members of the Crabb expedition, the Mexicans attempted to convince Americans that such activity was not only inadvisable, but also could be fatal. The threat must have been effective temporarily—no other American *filibusteros* attempted to enter Mexico during the remainder of the 1850s.

In the 1850s filibustering caused considerable difficulties between Mexico and the United States. Diplomatic correspondence between the United States ministers in Mexico and the United States secretary of state indicates that the Americans did not understand the Mexican position, and, in fact, did not deal honestly and fairly with Mexico. Consequently Mexico received mixed signals from the United States in respect to filibustering and American willingness to try to stop it. On the one hand, the United States had cooperated in completing the survey of the international boundary in 1853 and 1854 after the Gadsden Purchase Agreement. On the other hand there were many individuals both in and out of government in the United States who still wished to annex either Sonora or Baja California or both, and in the opinion of Mexicans the United States made no real effort to stop the raids of filibusters, Indians, or bandits who resided permanently north of the border. Mexican Secretary of Foreign Relations Lucas Alamán, for example, advised United States Minister to Mexico Alfred Conkling on May 17, 1853, that Raousset Boulbon had organized and led an armed party from the United States to invade Mexico "with the knowledge and permission of the authorities without any attempt on the part of the latter to prevent it as they might easily have done."[29] The next day, Conkling told Alamán that originally Raousset took a small party to Mexico "for a lawful and even praiseworthy purpose." That he "was very far from being convinced that the criminal acts he has indicated have, in this instance, been committed or if they have, that they are yet susceptible of proof."[30] One day later Conkling advised Secretary of State William L. Marcy that in the instance of Raousset the problem occurred as a consequence of Mexican behavior. Raousset, Conkling thought, had been duped.[31] Demonstrating a diplomacy of convenience rather than consistency, earlier in the month Conkling had told Marcy that José María Carvajal was a "notorious robber." He also told Alamán that the United States was sensitive to the problem, but that the laws of the country did not allow action unless proof was available; in addition witnesses must testify to the commission of a crime.[32]

In October 1856 the United States had sent John Forsyth to Mexico as its representative to inform the Mexican government that the United States had no sinister intentions. Forsyth communicated his message, but he also advised his government that Mexico would never achieve stability without direct United States intervention. When Forsyth complained about Mexican treatment of Juan N. Zerman and his men, Mexico responded that just because Zerman claimed to be helping one Mexican faction against another did not justify his meddling in its internal affairs and that the United States should have recognized that he was, in fact, trying to overthrow the legal government of Mexico. Mexico felt the same way about the Crabb expedition and believed that the United States had not sincerely tried to stop the activities.

Mexican officials also knew that public sentiment in the United States existed to intervene in Mexico. They knew, for example, that Senator Judah P. Benjamin of Louisiana had advocated that the U.S. acquire more Mexican territory, including Baja California. They suspected that in January 1858 United States President James Buchanan sanctioned filibustering when he publicly praised William Walker for his successful filibuster into Nicaragua. Finally, always on the alert to Texan opinion and actions, the Mexicans were aware that Senator Sam Houston had said during the late 1850s that the United States should establish a protectorate over Mexico and Central America. Thus, when Mexicans calculated the number of illegal expeditions launched amid such public approval and fanfare in the United States, they determined that the United States had not acted in good faith to stop filibustering, but, in fact, had an agenda detrimental to Mexican interests. One Mexico City newspaper editorialized that "we have seen the cunning and the means employed by the United States for the purpose of sowing among us the germ of discords, and by the side of this sinister conduct, would be beheld the simple credulity of a people which has called its enemy its brother, by going to the extreme of acknowledging as benefits the very injuries occasioned by its perfidy."[33] James Gadsden was still in Mexico negotiating the treaty to purchase more Mexican lands from Santa Anna's government, and Gadsden remained sensitive to difficulties between the governments. When Mexican officials complained about Raousset and Walker, Gadsden promised that the United States would act to stop such activities.[34] Yet Gadsden later told Marcy that newspapers in Mexico still charged that the United States "secretly instigated" many of the expeditions. Mexican writers described the United States actions as "barbaric and Gothic aggressions" that usually characterized the country's foreign policy toward Mexico.[35]

Whatever Gadsden might have said to the Mexicans, he was consistently critical of their government and leadership. On one occasion after he had negotiated the purchase treaty bearing his name, he advised Marcy that "the history of even the dark ages when government was identified with rude absolutism and cruel tyranny cannot point to a Dictatorship more deluded or more arbitrary and violent in its rules of sway."[36] Less than two years later, after Santa Anna's government had fallen and Juan Alvarez had provisionally occupied the presidency, Gadsden remarked that "the over awing or upsetting Alvarez's Government in the centre, will inevitably lead to the dismemberment of some six or seven northern states into a new federation seeking possibly ... annexation with the United States."[37]

Forsyth was becoming weary from all the negotiations caused by filibusters. He had no sooner put the Zerman problem aside when he heard of the arrival of the Henry Crabb expedition into Sonora. In April 1857, he told Lewis Cass, now secretary of state in the administration of James Buchanan, that "the Expeditionists have certainly chosen an unfortunate time for this movement as regards the interests of the United States in its relations with Mexico." He said he had tried to "eradicate from the Mexican mind, the deeply seated distrust of Americans, and to establish instead, a confidence in the friendly and honorable sentiments of our govt. and people towards them." He advised that Mexicans were still sensitive to what happened in Texas and California and feared loss of additional territory.[38] By June, Forsyth had heard that Crabb and

Henry Alexander Crabb *(courtesy of Arizona Historical Society, Tucson, #11693).*

James Buchanan *(from the collections of the Library of Congress, Washington, D.C.).*

his party had been captured and executed. He reported to Cass that in his opinion "there is little reason to doubt that Mr. Crabb was invited to Sonora and that he was the victim of deception, treachery, and surprise." In fact, he charged, Crabb was killed "to cover up the complicity and treason of some of the Mexican public men of Sonora. This is only surmise on my part, colored however by some dark hints that have come to me to that effect."[39]

Correspondence between Forsyth and the Mexican government continued. As the filibuster flurry began to settle down temporarily, Cass suggested to Forsyth that he approach the Mexicans about purchasing part of the northern frontier. This, of course, demonstrated how obtuse United States officials were in respect to alienation of any more Mexican territory. Forsyth had begun to understand Mexican attitudes toward such a proposal, and he told Cass that in his best judgment it was "impracticable and impossible" to gain more Mexican territory. He did approach the Mexican government, as Cass ordered him to, and then reported that

the present government of Mexico was pledged to the nation, in the strongest terms, not to alienate one foot of national territory. This proposition, so distasteful to this government, so wounding to its deep-seated pride, is backed by the offer of an equivalent in money, falling immensely below the exaggerated estimate which the government and the nation place upon the value of their National Domain accompanying the proposal for a new boundary. . . .[40]

In essence Forsyth understood the Mexican position, but, from time to time, believed that financial pressure on the various governments could lead to the purchase of more Mexican territory.[41] Forsyth also communicated this attitude to Mexican diplomats. The Mexican government responded angrily to Forsyth's hints of inherent problems in Mexico. The secretary of foreign relations advised him that all Mexico wanted was "nothing more for the maintenance of good relations with the U.S. than the observance of the principles of good neighborhood and impartial justice."[42] Thus, it was clear by the late 1850s that Mexico had become very defensive about its national sovereignty and that the United States refused to accept the position, believing instead that corrupt Mexican politicians could be persuaded by sufficient dollars.

The eve of the American Civil War brought one final filibustering scheme by U.S. opportunists. The organization of this effort grew out of a movement called the Knights of the Golden Circle, a pro-southern group that had as one of its far-reaching goals that of taking over Mexico and creating from it either a slave empire or an addition to the slave-holding South, thereby giving slave states the majority in the Union. In 1854 at Lexington, Kentucky, five men with grandiose ideas of pursuing such goals met and created the KGC. The primary organizer was George W. Bickley, originally of Indiana, who, with the help of a few like-minded men, determined to perpetuate slavery forever. The KGC thereafter grew slowly until the late 1850s, as the men organized clubs in southern states. They also established clubs in California and, perhaps, in Mexico.[43] The name of the organization originated with the plan to use Havana, Cuba, as the center of a great slave empire. Around Havana the men would draw a circle that included Maryland on the north, South America on the south, and extended to the West Indies. Within this great circle they would seek to control all the cotton, tobacco, rice, sugar, and coffee grown and sent to the U.S. The exports would be the financial basis of their empire.

The organizers of the KGC insisted publicly that their organization was not a filibustering effort. Whether its aims were clear or not, its structure was carefully laid out. Each person joining the group had to pay an initiation fee and swear allegiance to the organization. There were several divisions and one could be a member of a division based upon financial contribution and commitment. The Knights of the Iron Hand was the army of the organization; the financial arm was called the Knights of the True Faith; political control rested with the Governmental or Political Degree. Few persons could hold the last rank, and Bickley had a say in who joined the ruling clique. The organization was highly ritualistic and its goals changed during its existence. At one point the group claimed to support the liberal faction in Mexico against the conservative Miramón faction.

By 1860 many KGC clubs existed in Texas, with San Antonio having a large membership. At one time it was believed that Texas governor Sam Houston was a member, for he was known to have been in favor of the U.S. establishing a protectorate over Mexico. Houston, however, disavowed the organization when it became a secessionist association as the Civil War approached. He ordered the group disbanded in 1860. By March of 1860 rumors were rife in Texas that an invasion of Mexico was imminent. As many as 400 Knights were poised on the border near Brownsville prepared to cross the Río Bravo, but the invasion failed when many of the Knights left the staging area and returned to their homes. The plan collapsed because of the impending U.S. Civil War and internal conflicts in the KGC. The group evidently did not have the money to buy sufficient arms and ammunition to supply its erstwhile soldiers, and some members accused Bickley of absconding with the treasury. Whatever the truth, Bickley traveled to New Orleans and held a meeting of the faithful, but he was unsuccessful in uniting the organization. On May 7, 1860, the KGC met in Raleigh, North Carolina, where Bickley was temporarily forced to resign. He soon won back his position after exonerating himself of stealing funds.

Despite the protests of its members, the KGC also was clearly a racist organization. On September 12, 1859, Bickley said that the purpose of the group was "the invasion of a nation by a new and vigorous race— -the overthrow of old social systems, and the establishment of new ones—the disarming of hostile factions and the erection of peace establishments—the overthrow of prejudice, and the endoctrination [sic] of the people with new ideas of progress and prosperity."[44] As if this statement were not enough to establish the racist character of the organization, racism became even clearer when the editor of the *Dallas Herald* incited the Knights by writing, "Let these Texans range on the Mexican Frontier and infuse some of the Anglo Saxon ideas of progressiveness into the stupid leaden souls of that people."[45]

By the end of 1860 the KGC had evidently given up on the idea of its great circle of slavery and diverted its energies to the impending Civil War. Early in 1861 journalists learned more of the activities of the group. Some writers offered that the KGC had signed a colonization contract with Governor Manuel Doblado of Guanajuato, Mexico, in which the KGC would receive large land grants for supporting the governor. No evidence of this agreement is available. What did surface was that each member had to sign a pledge that he would support establishing a slave state in Mexico. Apparently no KGC members actually crossed the international border. Southern newspaper editors opined that Bickley only wanted to secure southern rights by perpetrating an American protectorate over Mexico. With Abraham Lincoln's election to the presidency, the KGC gave up its plans for Mexico and formed the core of Confederate troop organization in several seceding states.

Mexican authorities noted this filibustering plan, and, as usual, believed that the U.S. would take no action to stop it. Furthermore, Mexico continued to have problems with internal stability, French intervention, and filibustering while the Civil War raged north of the border.

5

1861-1889

nternal strife in Mexico after 1857 again made the country a fertile field for filibustering. The conflicts also weakened the position of Benito Juárez, who, as president, tried to reform and stabilize the country. Many clerics, soldiers, and wealthy elites who disagreed with Juárez's methods believed that only a return to a strong central government would stabilize the country and lead to economic development. Accordingly, some members of these groups supported a return to a monarchy, and this attitude was in concert with the desires of Napoleon III of France who cooperated with the individuals by sending General Frederick Forey and 36,000 troops to Mexico in the summer of 1863. Ostensibly the goal was to collect debts owed France. In reality the plan was to impose and support Austrian Archduke Maximilian as a puppet emperor of Mexico. Juárez and the liberals strongly opposed the intervention, but could do little to stop it. In late May 1864, Maximilian and his young wife Carlota arrived to assume the throne.[1] Juárez fled north to San Luis Potosí, then to the northern frontier from where he conducted steady guerrilla warfare against Maximilian's government. Early in 1867, Napoleon III withdrew his army and Maximilian's regime quickly collapsed. After Juárez captured and executed the emperor at Querétaro in May 1867 liberals again controlled Mexico.

Juárez wanted social and economic progress, but he seemed to be out of step with some who espoused progress through modernization and industrialization. Juárez died in 1872 and Sebastián Lerdo de Tejada became president. General Porfirio Díaz, who wanted stability and progress more than democratic freedoms, refused to accept Lerdo de Tejada's 1876 election and rebelled. Ultimately he made his base of operations at Brownsville, Texas. Díaz, leaning heavily upon *gringo* businessmen for help, overthrew Lerdo later that year. Díaz was born in Oaxaca (as was Juárez), had fought along-side Juárez against the French and identified with the liberal movement. Later, however, Díaz's personal views were essentially conservative. Díaz led his troops into Mexico City and occupied the presidency from 1876 until 1880. He stepped aside in 1880 and Manuel González became president, although Díaz was still the power behind the office. In 1884 Díaz returned to the presidency and several years later amended the constitution to allow himself to be reelected. He served until 1911 as a virtual dictator.[2] Conditions on the Mexican frontier between 1860 and 1889 again were sim-ilar to those of the entire country. Political squabbles, Indian and filibuster raids, and a poor economic environment characterized areas of the far north—conditions that encouraged filibustering. After 1860 Civil War in the United States forced the country to modify its attitudes and policies toward Mexico. Nonetheless, as the war began, the United States retained an interest in its neighbor to the south. Union leaders feared Confederate influ-ence or even invasion of Mexico by a foreign power. One American official recommended in 1861 that the United States purchase Baja California as it

is of no value to Mexico, its population does not exceed twelve thousand; a glance at the map will show its importance to us in a naval or military point of view in the event of an attack upon our Pacific possessions by any naval power or any attempt upon us or Mexico in that quarter by a lawless force.[3]

Although the French occupied much of Mexico during the Civil War, the U.S. was powerless to get them out of the country. Once the war ended, how-ever, United States authorities suggested to Napoleon III that he withdraw.

Despite the lasting problems of war and Reconstruction in the United States, there remained a latent spirit of expansionism. Mexican officials in the United States recognized this and believed the attitude posed a threat to their country's sovereignty. During the administrations of Andrew Johnson (1865-1869), and U. S. Grant (1869-1877), difficulties along the interna-tional border continued as Indians and filibusters raided on both sides. Neither the Johnson nor the Grant administrations was expansionist in respect to Mexico, but they did seek territory in areas then deemed of more immediate strategic or economic importance. William H. Seward, secretary of state in 1867, led the United States in acquiring Alaska and Midway Island in the Pacific Ocean. Seward hoped that eventually Hawaii would be added. In addition, Seward felt that the United States should exercise greater influence in the Caribbean. Grant agreed, thinking, for example, that the United States should acquire the Dominican Republic. During the years immediately after the Civil War, however, the public generally displayed little interest in expansion; Congress often reflected that mood.

By 1876, expansionist sentiment in respect to Mexico increased, and many individuals along the Texas-Mexican border manifested considerable interest in gaining a foothold in northern Mexico. Mexico, perhaps without knowing it, may have influenced some of the filibustering schemes after 1864 by attempting to entice colonists to immigrate. Mexican local and national authorities believed that if they followed the model of Argentina and other countries that recruited skilled settlers investors would help develop the country. One such effort was that of José María Iglesias, minister of development, who signed a contract with California rancher Jacobo P. Lease, a representative of the Compañía Colonizadora de la Baja California, to bring colonists to the region. The government offered land concessions as an incentive. Lease was supposed to pay for the contract but did not do so, and the government declared the agreement void in 1865. The next year a similar pact was signed between Lease and Mexican authorities, but the project also collapsed and was canceled. Between 1867 and 1876 other colonization contracts were signed, but failed to entice colonists. Still, individuals continued to immigrate south, and by 1876 there were approximately 25,000 foreigners living in Mexico. Most resided in the cities. In order to promote larger scale immigration through colonization schemes, Mexico modified its colonization laws in 1875, 1883, and 1894. Surely many of the characters north of the international border saw Mexico's actions as an opportunity, despite the fact that Mexico always specified it was not interested in *norteamericano* immigrants.[4]

U.S. businessmen were aware of Mexico's needs and financially encouraged Porfirio Díaz's revolution of Tuxtepec that began in 1876. James Stillman, son of Charles Stillman (who aided José María Carvajal in the 1850s), Mifflin Kennedy, Richard King, and others may have provided encouragement in money and guns. Díaz probably believed these men could help develop Mexico once he was firmly in power.

With the start of Rutherford B. Hayes' presidency in March 1877, problems between the United States and Mexico reflected a renewed spirit of expansionism. Hayes was at first hostile toward Díaz, but his position moderated on Díaz's assurance that he welcomed United States investment and on his avowed intention to take a strong stand concerning bandit raids that originated in Mexico and spilled over to the American side.[5] Part of the difficulty between Díaz and Hayes related also to the fact that in April 1877, General E. O. C. Ord, United States Army commander of the Department of Texas, learned that two Mexican guides who had helped the army against the Lipan Apaches in Mexico had been arrested by authorities in Piedras Negras. The Mexican officials intended to execute the two and refused to discuss the matter. Ord ordered a detachment to cross the border to rescue the prisoners. The attempt failed, but Mexicans interpreted the border crossing as a violation of Mexican sovereignty and a blatant intervention in Mexican affairs. After 1878 Díaz agreed to limited border crossing reciprocity and during the 1880s signed treaties to legalize the cross-border incursions in pursuit of bandits.

Hayes sought to use Mexico's unwillingness or inability to stop raids originating in Mexico as ample reason to order troops across the line whenever it seemed appropriate. Díaz ordered General Jerónimo Treviño, Ord's future son-in-law, then in command of the Mexican troops on the northern border, to stop bandits or others who launched invasions of the United States from Mexico and to oppose any United States troops who crossed the line. Much of the anti-American maneuvering was posturing intended for Mexican consumption; in truth Díaz usually dealt easily and quietly with U.S. officials.

Still, some Mexicans took things at face value and saw Hayes' directive to Ord as opening the path to a new invasion of Mexican territory. Relations between the two countries were strained temporarily because of the border instability and Hayes' unwillingness to recognize the Díaz government. Fortunately, no armed conflict occurred between the two armies. Banditry, however, on both sides of the international line remained a problem.

During the administrations of Republicans James A. Garfield and Chester A. Arthur (1881-1885) and Democrat Grover Cleveland (1885-1889 and 1893-1897), the United States did pursue an openly expansionist policy regarding Mexican territory. Political and economic changes were taking place in the United States that would encourage a revival of such sentiments.

Most of the talk concerned opportunity for investment. During the summer of 1883, several wealthy businessmen met in New York City to discuss railroads and mining in Mexico, as well as the possibility of acquiring such areas as the frontier state of Chihuahua. Sentiment for separating parts of northern Mexico had not died. Benjamin Harrison, a Republican, assumed the presidency in 1889, and again the United States had a leader with expansionist notions. He appointed James G. Blaine, who had a particular interest in Latin America and in expansion in general, secretary of state. The mood of the United States government can be seen in its aspirations to acquire Hawaii and to establish naval bases in or near Latin America. As the imperialism of the 1890s gained momentum, it was once again tainted with ideas of *gringo* racial superiority. The tone was not Manifest Destiny but a desire on the part of Americans to build a colonial empire whose populations would remain subject to and inferior to *gringos*.[6]

Between 1861 and 1889 several American adventurers or entrepreneurs schemed to enter Mexico as "colonizers" or made no pretext to be anything but filibusters. Most of the expeditions never entered Mexico. They were planned, apparently well organized, but miscarried because of inept leadership. Despite the failures, the ventures were filibustering attempts that the Mexican government took seriously. From the activities of the organizers—as reported in newspapers and in messages to Mexican diplomats in the United States—Mexicans gained an even clearer understanding of the attitudes of many United States citizens and their government toward acquiring more territory through filibustering and intervention.

Public opinion and official positions in the United States notwithstanding, filibustering continued. In March 1861, on the eve of the first shots fired in the Civil War, Mexican officials advised the United States government that a filibustering expedition had been organized in San Francisco and had already departed for Baja California. John B. Weller, United States envoy extraordinary and minister plenipotentiary in Mexico City, had learned of the campaign when the Mexican secretary of foreign relations gave him documents from officials in Baja California and Sonora concerning the affair. According to the documents, the filibusters would invade Baja California, then Sonora, and ultimately Sinaloa. Weller told the Mexican government that the United States would investigate the matter and he suggested that Mexico punish severely any illegal *entradas* whether by filibusters or colonizers.[7] The Mexican official replied that the United States should stop any expedition before it was launched. If not, Mexico would show no mercy toward intruders.[8]

Meanwhile, violation of Mexican territory had already taken place. In early March, Captain José Moreno arrived in Baja California with 200 men—mostly Americans but including some Mexicans—and immediately confronted the forces of Governor Feliciano R. de Esparza. After one brief fight, the *filibusteros* fled hurriedly across the border to safety.[9] On March 5, Secretary of State William H. Seward advised Mexican authorities that his government was not guilty of overlooking filibustering expeditions organized in the United States.[10] Seward suggested that the filibusters were Mexicans dissatisfied with local rule. Maintaining good relations with Mexico became more significant to the United States each month. In June, President Abraham Lincoln promised that he would do all he could to stop filibustering.[11] By this time Lincoln wanted no problems with Mexico. He was deeply involved in mobilizing the United States to deal with the newly seceded Confederate states.[12]

In August, American authorities learned from Mexico that Confederate Colonel Earl Van Dorn had left San Antonio, Texas, en route to El Paso and to Baja California. Evidently Mexico believed that Van Dorn and his 1300 men were going to attack. Lincoln advised the Mexicans that he had ordered General E. V. Sumner, commanding the Military Division of the Pacific, to be watchful for any Confederate troop movement toward Baja California. There was, however, nothing Sumner could do about Confederate activities in Texas at the time. By the end of 1861 the Mexicans realized that complaining about filibustering activities that might originate in the Confederacy was pointless.

Even while the Civil War raged, Americans in California still looked longingly at the Mexican frontier. Some even believed that because the United States was so involved in the war their opportunities were even better. Seeing the distraction as an opportunity, William McKendree Gwin, a southerner and ex-California senator, promoted and planned with the help of the French government a scheme with himself as "The Duke of Sonora."

Born in Tennessee in 1805, Gwin was educated at Transylvania University in law and medicine and practiced medicine in Mississippi. He lived briefly in New Orleans before moving to California. He arrived in San Francisco in

June of 1849 and participated in writing the state constitution. In 1850, he went to Washington as a senator from California. He remained in Washington most of the time until 1861, when he returned to a plantation he owned in Mississippi.[13] During the winter of 1862-1863, he journeyed to France aboard the blockade runner *Robert E. Lee*. Gwin had a proposal for French monarch Napoleon III.[14] Gwin would colonize Sonora and exploit the gold and silver mines there for his own benefit and that of the French ruler. The Marquis de Montholon, Napoleon III's minister to Mexico, thought Gwin's proposal a solid one and encouraged the French monarch to support it. With Montholon's assistance, Gwin met with Maximilian, who proved less than enthusiastic about the American's scheme. Gwin also met with Count Mercier, the French minister of foreign affairs, who was more impressed with the plan.[15]

In January 1864, with Mercier's help, Gwin presented his scheme to Napoleon III, who expressed interest. The plan apparently offered possible wealth and the means to control more of Mexico.[16] Count Mercier also won the interest of the Duc de Morny, Napoleon III's half brother and most influential advisor. De Morny was interested in investing money in the venture, and he agreed that Gwin would receive the title of "Duke of Sonora." Shortly thereafter, Napoleon III discussed the proposal with Maximilian, who agreed to meet again with Gwin. Although Maximilian was somewhat cool, he did not reject the idea and admitted that it might be feasible. The response was significant enough encouragement for Gwin to prepare for his first trip to Mexico, especially since Napoleon III had given Gwin a letter to present to Marshal Bazaine, French military commander in Mexico.

Emperor Maximilian and Empress Carlota embarked for Mexico on April 14, 1864; Gwin followed two weeks later. On reaching Mexico City, Gwin went to see Marshal Bazaine, who was not particularly friendly toward him.[17] Moreover, Gwin's documents commending him to Maximilian had some how gotten lost and the new emperor used this fact as reason enough to refuse to see him. Gwin recognized that there was more to Maximilian's refusal than the mere absence of proper documents.

In despair, Gwin wrote to the Duc de Morny to encourage him to make certain that no orders stopping the scheme had been issued from Paris. Gwin tried to obtain Bazaine's attention long enough to get some assistance but the fifty-five-year-old military commander was busy courting a seventeen-year-old Mexican girl and had no desire to get involved with Gwin.[18] Moreover, Maximilian made it clear that he had absolutely no intention of helping an American adventurer who had designs on Mexico. Maximilian had convinced himself that the Mexicans loved him; under such circumstances he saw himself as the guardian of the country. Gwin spent several months in Mexico City trying to get an audience with the emperor, but Maximilian still refused to see him. Again Gwin turned to France, complaining to Napoleon III that Maximilian and Bazaine would not assist him. Napoleon III responded by urging Maximilian to cooperate with Gwin. Carlota did agree to see Gwin, and after he explained his plan, apparently consented to help. Apparently, she could get no support from Maximilian either. She never advised Gwin what the result of her intercession had been.[19]

Gwin saw Maximilian informally at a wedding a few days later and learned that the emperor had no intention of helping. As a last resort, on January 19, 1865, Gwin sailed for France hoping to get Napoleon III to order the French military in Mexico to help him. Four days after his arrival in Paris, his strongest supporter in Napoleon III's cabinet, the Duc de Morny, died, signaling the end of Gwin's influence with Napoleon III. Gwin, however, finally got an audience with the Emperor and again convinced him of the potential for wealth on the Mexican frontier. Napoleon III was intrigued with Gwin's presentation and gave him a note to Bazaine ordering the French military commander to cooperate in the venture.[20]

On January 31, 1865, Gwin sailed for Mexico where he learned that his only ally in the country, the Marquis de Montholon, had been transferred to Washington. Now Gwin had no one in Mexico who would talk to him. He presented Napoleon III's note to Marshal Bazaine, but the French commander merely scoffed at him, stating unceremoniously that he would not cooperate under any circumstances.[21] With no assistance coming, Gwin departed for the United States late in the summer of 1865. He arrived at San Antonio and was immediately arrested by the United States military authorities. United States officials had watched his scheming for several years. In 1864 United States Minister to Mexico William Corwin had told Seward that Gwin apparently wished to colonize Sonora, but that Maximilian did not support the plan. In fact, the Emperor and "the great majority of the Mexicans are decidedly opposed to this scheme of immigration—fearing, as they do, more than all things else, the Americans of the North."[22] Gwin was not released from jail until May 1866; by then he had abandoned his dream of becoming the "Duke of Sonora." He returned to Mississippi where he remained until his death in 1885.[23] The Gwin episode occasioned considerable diplomatic correspondence between the United States and Mexico and between the United States and France. The United States, however, was more concerned with getting the French out of Mexico and had already begun to pressure Napoleon III to withdraw his support for Maximilian.[24]

After 1865 still other adventurers schemed to take Mexican territory. Most of the plans included annexing territory to the United States. During 1865 a group of men organized the Lower California Homestead Association in San Francisco. They incorporated with $40,000 capital stock and made no attempt to conceal the fact that they intended to enter Mexico in whatever fashion possible. The expedition never crossed the border, however, and in 1866 the organizers abandoned their scheme—at least for that year. In July 1867 rumors circulated that filibusters were reorganizing the Lower California Homestead Association in New York City and in New Orleans.[25] Rumor had it that some enterprising men had gathered 50,000 volunteers for the venture. This time United States authorities ordered General Philip Sheridan to make certain that the army was prepared to intervene should an armed party attempt to cross the border. As usual the secretary of the Mexican legation in Washington, in this instance Matías Romero, advised W. H. Seward that Mexico was disturbed about the newest threat.[26]

Romero, born in Oaxaca in 1837, served Mexico as a diplomat in the United States during several decades of filibustering. He was a friend both of Benito Juárez and Porfirio Díaz. Like Juárez and Díaz, he graduated from the Instituto de Ciéncias y Artes in Oaxaca. He commenced his career in politics in 1855 when he moved to Mexico City and began work as a clerk in the foreign relations office. He entered training for law and on the recommendation of his close friend, Ignacio Mariscal, was admitted to the bar in 1857. Romero studied English and French and learned to speak English fluently. On November 23, 1859, he received his first assignment in Washington, D.C., when he became secretary of the Mexican Legation. In 1868 he married the younger sister of William E. Allen, an Ohio congressman, and returned to Mexico to become secretary of hacienda, a post he held until 1872. He remained in Mexico ten years but carried on a long correspondence with many of his American friends.

Ignacio Mariscal *(courtesy Archivo Historico
de las Relaciones Exteriores, México, D.F.).*

Matías Romero *(courtesy Archivo Historico
de las Relaciones Exteriores, México, D.F.).*

Romero returned to hacienda in 1878. He served until Díaz appointed him minister to Washington on February 2, 1882. In this position he always demonstrated his patience and friendship toward the United States. In fact, many Mexicans believed that he had spent so much time north of the Río Bravo that he was out of touch with Mexico. In reality he was strongly pro-Mexican, but he knew his country and the United States better than almost anyone of his generation. He opposed filibustering or any form of United States intervention as vigorously as possible.[27]

Romero argued that after 1865 the United States had made an effort to stop filibustering. On many occasions he explained to his countrymen the legal problems that United States authorities faced in such matters. During filibustering activity in the late 1860s, he notified his government that the United States would cooperate to stop such border violations and would alert troops to investigate any suspicious activity. He also related that acting United States Attorney John M. Binkley would investigate rumors of new filibustering efforts.[28] These filibustering expeditions never left the United States, but they alerted the Mexicans, now that the Civil War was over, about potential threats from north of the border. The episode also occasioned much discussion between the two governments. As had always been the case, newspapers in several sections of the country carried long reports of filibustering activities. Romero and other Mexican officials in the United States learned of most schemes from Mexican consuls who sent newspapers from California or Texas to both the legation and the central government in Mexico City. Mexicans still could not understand why the United States stood idly by while entrepreneurs publicly organized illegal expeditions.

Filibustering activities continued, however. In January 1871, another group busily organized near Tucson, Arizona, to invade Chihuahua and Sonora. These men reportedly planned to establish a new country they would call "La República del Pacífico," ultimately including Baja California. Rumors prevailed on both sides of the border that 1500 men would soon leave Chicago for Arizona and then on to Mexico. Approximately 500 Texans were to gather at El Paso while 2500 others were to depart from an unspecified location in California.

Mexicans were well aware of this activity; it was reported in detail in the newspapers from several cities in the United States and in Mexican towns along the border. In Sonora, a state in which American privateers were interested, Mexicans frequently learned of filibustering through frequent ship traffic from California to Guaymas. Reports included information that filibusters believed that Mexicans in all the states would welcome them as saviors from an unstable and corrupt government. That sentiment might have been true for a minority, but most Mexicans disliked Americans meddling in their affairs. Mexicans did not have detailed information concerning the activities of the party called La República del Pacífico. According to some newspaper reports, the leader of the group was a "General" Banning from California, who owned property in Sonora. In view of what had happened since the 1846-1848 struggle with the U.S., Mexican authorities took the threats of these and other expeditions seriously. As a result, Mexico tried to keep adequate troops stationed on the frontier.[29] Despite all the preparations that evidently took place to get Banning's expedition underway, it never entered Mexico. Either newspaper coverage of the activities or Mexican preparation for defense caused the organizers to give up or delay their plans.

La República del Pacífico members might have been involved in a similar scheme in 1871 and 1872. Rumors prevailed again that a group of filibusters from California were preparing to capture Baja California. The men claimed they were going to Baja California to work the saline deposits in the middle of the peninsula. Newspapers in California often mentioned business ventures of this type during the period. Commercial entrepreneurs usually hoped to get help from local Mexican officials by involving them in the schemes. Frequently, however, many of these quasi-legitimate business ventures were merely covers for more nefarious schemes to annex territory.

One such group arrived in Baja California on July 29, 1871, but did not go immediately to mines or saline deposits. In fact, months passed before the party finally got to the mines. According to Mexican reports, the adventurers were actually *filibusteros* headed by Charles J. Jausen of San Francisco. Jausen claimed that the Mexican consul in San Francisco had given him permission to enter Mexico to work the salt deposits. Jausen and his party arrived at the saline deposits late in 1871 and began mining. Jausen claimed to have extracted 1300 tons of salt between July 1871 and December 1872. Mexican authorities opposed these commercial efforts, however, and again saw the action as a precurser to settlement and perhaps loss of the territory. The situation was further complicated when Mexican officials found that the ship Jausen had chartered to take his group to Guaymas had been involved in an attack on the Sonoran city. Jausen denied any part in the fighting and claimed that his efforts were entirely legitimate.[30] In 1874 government officials sent troops to Baja California and forced Jausen out of the country.[31]

These activities provoked considerable difficulties between the United States and Mexico. Mexican authorities believed that the United States government once again had encouraged filibustering by not enforcing its neutrality laws. Mexicans claimed, in fact, that rumors abounded that the United States actually supported filibustering, and that the country had eight gunboats on the Mississippi River poised for an attack should any filibusters gain a foothold in Mexico. Although the report was untrue, Mexicans believed it possible and remained convinced that the United States was really behind most of the schemes. Some Mexicans suggested that the only way to deal with frontier problems relating to filibustering, Indian attacks, and bandit raids originating north of the border was to declare war on the United States.[32]

Rumors of new filibustering expeditions reached Mexico again early in 1873. Another group was organizing in Tucson, Arizona, to invade Chihuahua and Sonora. Mexicans had heard from sources in the United States that capitalists in New York City and San Francisco were financing the venture.[33] Early the next year Mexican officials in the capital confirmed that Alexander D. Hamilton, former treasurer of Jersey City, New Jersey, had arrived at Matamoros, Mexico, with city funds and was going to use the money to finance a filibustering campaign. United States government officials filed charges against Hamilton and asked Mexico to extradite him. Several newspapers in the U.S. ran articles relating that Hamilton was involved in a filibustering scheme similar to that of Carvajal earlier. Hamilton had heard of Carvajal's effort and wanted to revive the idea of carving a new country called the Republic of the Sierra Madre out of northern Mexico. Some Mexican leaders accused Juan N. Cortina of Matamoros and other Mexicans of assisting Hamilton.[34] This might have been true. Hamilton eventually turned himself in to New Jersey authorities, claiming that he had done nothing wrong other than to become involved with Cortina. In fact, he later claimed that Cortina had hidden him in his personal residence, where Hamilton overheard Cortina offer to sell him to American authorities for $20,000. Hamilton escaped out of the back door and fled to the United States.[35] The Mexican government issued orders to governors of the frontier states to arrest Hamilton if he could be found. Hamilton failed to organize an expedition, but his activities again prompted diplomatic exchanges.[36]

Tucson, Arizona Territory (above), was often the jumping-off point for filibustering expeditions. Below, Tucson's Congress Hall Saloon, gathering place for men like Grant Oury *(both photos courtesy Arizona Historical Society, Tucson, #s 30125 and 20858).*

Authorities in the United States were aware of the rumors of Hamilton's impending filibuster and pledged to station 50,000 troops along the border to stop it. Such pledges for troops had never been kept. Many officials in the United States believed also that Mexicans were involved in the plan because they were weary of the instability of the Mexican government and long-term neglect of frontier issues by the officials in Mexico City.

Whether Hamilton represented ambitious American investors or whether he was simply an eccentric is not known. Nevertheless, many entrepreneurs from the United States wanted to establish various industries, build railroads, and create a free-trade zone in northern Mexico and it is possible that one of the investors suggested the scheme to Hamilton. Regardless of who was responsible, U.S. news reports of such activities created considerable concern in Mexico. Either because of a shortage of financial support in the United States or as a consequence of the wide-spread publicity warning the Mexicans, the plotters dropped their plan. Some of the participants undoubtedly retained their interest and attempted to attach themselves to later filibustering schemes.[37]

In 1875, slightly less than a year after the Hamilton episode, rumors spread that another group of *gringos* were preparing an expedition near the mouth of the Nueces River in Texas. More than 100 men reportedly were armed and ready to enter Mexico. A Mr. Weber, who was known locally as a *mal hombre*, supposedly was behind this new scheme. According to those who claimed to know about the intent of the group, it was said that Weber had decided to attack Piedras Negras, across from Eagle Pass, Texas, and use the town as a base to spread the operation throughout northern Mexico.[38] Mexican authorities learned of the venture and sent General Carlos Fuero, Jefe de Colonias Militares del Estado, with troops to expel the intruders. Again the filibustering expedition failed to get underway on any significant scale, although newspapers reported that on at least one occasion Weber actually had crossed the Río Bravo into Mexico and attacked a large hacienda.[39]

Continuing rumors of impending invasion from the north kept Mexicans constantly on the alert. Authorities in Mexico City were aware that many past rumors were unsubstantiated, but they still believed that *filibusteros* could ultimately constitute a genuine threat to the country's sovereignty. Public opinion as expressed in Mexico City newspapers can be seen clearly in an editorial of March 17, 1877, published in the *Monitor Republicano*. This editorial suggested that the paper had

published the absurd opinions of two of our colleagues of the American Press, first, in order to show our countrymen the danger which threatens us from filibustering tendencies of our neighbors of the north; second in order to warn the government of the necessity of avoiding on the frontier all pretexts for provoking an international conflict. We do not give to the article published greater importance than they deserve, since, from long and attentive observation, we know that the American press, is in its greater part, simply the interested voice of speculation, or the intemperate organ of political parties; but we must confess that the projects for the gradual absorption of the Mexican territory receive daily greater favor in what we call the Sister Republic.

The editor added that the Democratic Party in the United States had always been expansionist, and that sentiment had not changed. But the Democratic party was not alone in its sentiments. Mexicans believed that while he was president U. S. Grant also was involved in a scheme to establish a protectorate over Mexico.[40] Perception of threats from the United States and the fact that Mexican officials believed the United States unwilling to respect its sovereignty contributed as always to tense relations between the two countries.[41]

Some talk of filibustering never posed a serious threat and merely grew out of rumors about Porfirio Díaz's struggle to take control of the government. Mexicans involved in filibustering schemes might have been opponents of Díaz, but Americans recognized the opportunities Mexican instability promoted and they often planned publicly to take advantage. One expedition that combined Mexican opponents of Díaz and American filibusters was organized during the 1870s, allegedly to assist Sebastián Lerdo de Tejada against Díaz.[42] In reality, American adventurers attempted to use Lerdo de Tejada's name to help them establish a foothold, after which they would annex northwestern Mexico. Eighteen hundred men in San Francisco volunteered to join the effort. Local newspapers suggested that ultimately 3000 men would be involved. The plan called for more than 1000 of the men to sail to Guaymas and capture the port city, while another 500 would gather at Fort Yuma and from there attack overland into northern Sonora. An additional 500 men from El Paso would attack Chihuahua City. As Mexico had no more than 500 poorly armed federal troops stationed along the frontier, success seemed plausible. Mexican troops were almost constantly engaged in fighting Indians who raided across the border from the United States, further complicating their task. One of the organizers of the expedition was Vaughn Thomas, or "General" as he referred to himself, a veteran of William Walker's Nicaraguan venture. James D. Poston, a Quaker and longtime frontiersman who had extensive ranching interests in Mexico and was well known in the region, was also an instigator.

The United States government was aware of filibustering activity and ordered General E. O. C. Ord to send troops to the border to stop the expedition. Mexican General Manuel Gonzáles, comandante en jefe de la Armada del Pacífico y de las Fuerzas de Occidente, also prepared troops in Baja California to repulse the invasion.[43] Once again, either because the Mexicans appeared well organized to fight or because of other problems, the group did not enter Mexico, falling apart before its leaders could get the men south. Mexican officials, again reading of this expedition in California and other border newspapers, could not understand why the United States tolerated the activity, prompting more hostility on the part of Mexicans toward the United States. U.S. officials in Mexico sensed "a growing bitterness of feeling towards the United States and a general belief that a war between the two countries is almost inevitable."[44] In fact, the countries were debating frontier troubles when Díaz sent more troops to the Río Bravo.

In the midst of negotiations over such items as border crossing reciprocity, chasing bandits, hostile Indians, or filibusters, rumors surfaced that American citizens actually tried to start a war with Mexico in an attempt to seize more territory. Captain L. H. McNelly, a Texas Ranger, and Lieutenant Commander Dewitt C. Kells of the gunboat *U.S.S. Río Bravo* stationed at the mouth of the river, plotted a shooting incident with Mexican troops that would start the conflict. The effort failed when the United States government—this time acting quickly—discovered the plan and relieved Kells of his command.[45]

Another well-publicized scheme—both in Mexico and the United States—was that of Ernest Dalrymple. Dalrymple, a forty-six-year-old fanatic from Pennsylvania, attempted to organize an expedition between 1877 and 1880. Dalrymple wanted to lead his expedition south when, on June 1, 1877, Rutherford B. Hayes withdrew United States troops charged with controlling conditions along the border. Dalrymple advertised in local newspapers calling for 50,000 volunteers for a "Grand Army of Occupation."

He intended to use Civil War veterans to help him annex all of Mexico and eventually Central America. Dalrymple printed and distributed advertisements and circulars, showing a racial bias that was rampant in Texas and California. He wrote that "a people incapable of appreciating the gifts of nature, who were without the capacity for self-goverment, must receive the unwelcome assistance of their superiors." Dalrymple and his associate, Alfred Van Riswick, designed an invasion flag and passed out silk badges the color of the flag to all men who would join the effort.[46] He then issued a proclamation about Mexico that caused additional concern. "Behold a vision," he said, "of enchantment, a continent pulled by the waves of two oceans, slumbering. Centuries of mis-rule weigh down her eye-lids—she lies naked among her riches. Tell me brothers! Who shall awake the Queen and adorn her with civilization? Shall it be the European, fettered with royalty, or shall it be you, the free American?"[47] Such grandiose pronouncements did not escape the notice of Mexican officials.

In May 1880 Dalrymple guaranteed great economic rewards to all who joined his enterprise. He generously promised everyone who helped him that he would redeem Mexican bonds held in Europe and grant "limited monopolies" to his subordinates. Dalrymple proposed to pay his soldiers with lands, bonds, and future civil-service positions. He suggested that his success in Mexico would provide the United States with $100,000,000 in Mexican trade each year. He also publicly proclaimed that the population of Mexico was a "miserable lot of people; that they took the country from some other races and really have no . . . right to it."[48] Dalrymple claimed that he had received support from adventurers in California, Arizona, and Texas. His associates were busily recruiting, in fact, in Austin and in several other cities. "General" F. M. James of the Texas state militia was enlisting volunteers for the effort. In fact, the recruiter was "General" James A. Corbs, commander of Dalrymple's Grand Army of the Republic and a brigadier in the Texas militia. He reportedly raised 500 eager men in Austin.[49]

Newspaper coverage of Dalrymple's adventure helped his efforts. Editors published his pronouncements and in some instances gave approval to his plan. One California writer referred to him as "the champion warrior of the glorious nineteenth century who wishes to conquer Mexico and inaugurate the millenium in the land of the Aztecs."[50] Newspaper accounts of Mexico and its supposed weaknesses at this time also encouraged the ventures. One author wrote that

there are a great many intelligent Mexicans in Sonora and other border states who have found that the mere sentiment of patriotism has been fruitless in that country. They want a new Era of Prosperity. Such a man as ex-governor Pesqueira of Sonora would shed no tears if he saw the state transferred to the Federal Union. When American interests predominate in Sonora and other northern states, what then? The logic of events would finally be a transfer of sovereignty, and this perhaps without any violence or loss of friendly feeling.[51]

Occasionally an editor would harshly criticize filibustering. One wrote that extending the boundaries of the United States at Mexican expense was not "right, proper, or pardonable." To this man such expeditions would seem as if "robbery, simple and reckless, was now the motive for this contemplated invasion of a friendly neighbor's territory."[52] General William T. Sherman expressed clearly the view of the United States Army when he wrote that "there is no longer any cause for invasion of Mexico. Slavery could not be introduced there even if the invasion were made and it proved successful. If that be the object, it is a foolish proposition."[53]

The few newspapermen who expressed dismay at and opposed filibustering and Sherman's feelings did not provoke a change in attitude. Concluding that Dalrymple's scheme was a threat that could result in yet another attempt to take more territory, the Mexican government remained fearful of American support for the activities.[54] An angry official suggested that "The excitable Texans, who are always ready for anything relating to a piratical war against a neighboring country, have received with visible enthu-siasm the call of Dalrymple and have immediately begun to affiliate them-selves under the 'banner of the free.'"[55] One Mexican official advised the gov-ernor of Texas that the Dalrymple plot would create a

disturbance that is liable to produce in the reciprocal feeling of amity and cordiality that the prudence of the government of the two nations has been building up among the popular masses of their respective people. There is among your people, if not a decided tendency, at least a marked predisposi-tion to enterprises of that kind even under such a barbarian policy as filibustering.[56]

By 1880 it had become clear that Dalrymple was not going to succeed. His inability to execute the plan and the threat of confrontation with United

States Army troops along the border under E.O.C. Ord caused many volunteers to abandon the effort. Mexican officials also had watched the group carefully and had sent additional troops to the frontier to meet any invasion. Moreover, Ord was sympathetic to the Mexicans; his daughter had recently married the son of General Jerónimo Treviño, a division commander.

Early in September 1880, with armed forces on both sides of the border prepared to intercept him, Dalrymple's expedition collapsed and he reluctantly gave up. Mexicans remained convinced, however, that the United States secretly coveted Mexican territory, and that the only way to stop filibusters was for the United States to punish men like Dalrymple severely.[57] In response to what happened to Dalrymple, the United States advised Mexican authorities that Dalrymple had broken no laws and that he had not actually led an expedition from the United States into Mexico. He had only talked about doing so. The response further convinced Mexicans that the United States, by abdication of its authority at least, approved of the outlawry.

The diplomatic dust from the Dalrymple fiasco had scarcely settled in 1886 when Mexican officials learned of a new threat. A group calling itself the MarVista League hoped to put together another expedition into Mexico. The leaders proposed to establish the state of MarVista in Baja California, widely advertising their intent in California newspapers and offering shares in the project for twenty-five cents each. According to the organizers, share holders would be entitled to vote to create the state. All anyone needed to do to be a citizen was to own "a shotgun, saddle pony, and twenty-four hours residence." One of the prominent organizers was Tomás Valdespino Figueroa, a shawdowy figure from San Diego about whom little is known.[58] The promoters of this scheme said they were interested in exploiting the silver and gold mines of Baja California and later would widen their influence to take in all of the region. Mexican authorities compared the venture to that of William Walker and did not believe the group alone constituted any immediate danger to Mexico. Nonetheless they watched the group's activities and advised the United States government of their concern. Evidently the filibusters failed to launch an attack and in late 1886, as support on both sides of the border evaporated, the venture disintegrated.[59]

By this time another potentially dangerous filibustering expedition was being organized. A. K. Cutting of New Mexico, a typesetter and newspaper man well-known in Texas, northwestern Mexico, and in New Mexico as a "dead beat" with occasional business dealings in Juárez, planned to lead a party into Mexico and seek revenge against the government. According to Cutting, Mexican authorities had jailed him for no reason while he was in the country. He vowed reprisals.[60] On his return to New Mexico, he told his story to newspapers. Editors along the border enthusiastically printed the story and remarked that such abuses of liberty were the usual fare south of the border. The editors warned that Americans who strayed across the line should be aware of the danger.

The editor of the Santa Fe *Daily New Mexican,* probably of Mexican ancestry, was almost alone in his criticism of Cutting when he wrote that the *gringo* had no business interfering in Mexico, and that "the fire of kindred blood burns in our veins, and we resent as personal insults the abusive language used by the Democratic press toward the government and citizens of old Mexico. We shall never forget that it was the home of our ancestors and is the home of our kinsfolk." The same writer ran the comments of a United States Army officer in Washington who publicly stated that war with Mexico would not be as easy as last time, for "the mongrel half-Indian population make very good soldiers in many ways. While they are not the equal of the Anglo-Saxon in stamina and staying qualities, they can out march any infantry I ever saw."[61] Cutting probably shared the same racial attitude.

Cutting claimed that Mexico owed him indemnity for falsely incarcerating him, and once he was back in New Mexico took his claim first to the United States House of Representatives and ultimately to President Grover Cleveland. Neither responded.

The Santa Fe *Daily New Mexican* of August 17, 1886, carried more about Cutting. According to the editor, Cutting had lived for a while in El Paso and had become involved in unspecified illegal activity in Ciudad Juárez that led him before a Mexican judge. Cutting repented and told the judge he would cause no more trouble. He was set free. Evidently Cutting reentered Mexico illegally shortly afterward and was again jailed. He was released and returned to the United States.[62]

In fact, Cutting's problem with Mexican authorities stemmed from his public battle with E. G. Medina, a Ciudad Juárez resident. Medina charged that Cutting had defamed him in an article written for an El Paso newspaper. Medina sued Cutting and Mexican law prescribed the libel as a misdemeanor punishable by up to two years in jail and a fine of from $300 to

$2000. Cutting made the mistake of returning to Mexico and publicly announcing that Mexicans had no authority over him. Officials promptly arrested him. Cutting appealed to the United States consul in Ciudad Juárez—J. Harvey Brigham. Brigham demanded Cutting's release and the case became a diplomatic matter. Henry R. Jackson, United States minister to Mexico, advised Ignacio Mariscal, Mexican secretary of foreign relations, that Cutting was lodged in a "loathsome and dirty" jail and should immediately be released.[63] The official U.S. report on the Cutting case was a sixty-seven page document detailing the events and blaming Mexico for the problem. The Mexican government responded with a lengthy document accusing the United States of meddling in its internal affairs.

The Mexicans then decided to make public all they knew of Cutting. Officials claimed that Cutting wanted to get even with Mexico. He had promised publicly that he would organize and lead a filibustering expedition into the country. He claimed in a statement published in local newspapers that he was organizing against the "corrupt, rotten and tottering Mexican government, not against the Mexican people."[64] He bragged that he had the support of wealthy men from New York and even from the Mormon Church. Cutting said that as soon as he got 7000 recruits signed up, his backers would advance the necessary funds. He offered that Mexico had 10,000,000 people most of whom were "full blood Indians, ignorant and oppressed beyond measure."[65]

Whether Cutting had any financial promises is not known. He had sent recruiters to several cities; two men arrived in Dallas, Texas, and told local reporters that Cutting had established an executive committee of twelve men. He claimed to have the support of three businessmen from El Paso, three others who were Roman Catholic priests, and others who were wealthy Utah and New York City men. Cutting's enterprise received considerable publicity, especially in Texas; recruiting, however, was not good.[66] He appealed to all sorts of fanatics, suggesting that he was going to create a "Socialistic Republic," out of the three states of Sonora, Coahuila, and Chihuahua. He planned to abolish peonage, and to divide the haciendas, giving 200-acre tracts to peasants. He offered the Catholic church the restoration of its lands lost during the Juárez era, and offered Mormons settlers "absolute self government." He would restore freedom of speech and press in Mexico, establish a compulsory education system, allow free entry of goods from the United States, and place a prohibitive tariff on goods from England, France, and Germany.[67]

Mexican authorities believed Cutting posed no immediate threat, but they feared that his rhetoric and the general attitude of Americans toward Mexico might encourage others to help him or to organize their own efforts. They also read the racist remarks and feared that such bravado north of the border would stir up general support for United States intervention in Mexico. The Mexican government protested Cutting's actions in several diplomatic notes to the United States, indicating that such activities again threatened to destroy the good relations between the two countries. Some in the United States agreed with Mexican sentiment that Cutting posed no threat to Mexico. One newsman referred to the affair as a "Texan Dime Novel," and made fun of Cutting's attempt to incorporate "the socialistic and communistic pagans within the pale of the Roman Church."[68]

Despite publicity and the attitude of citizens on both sides of the border, Cutting renewed his efforts and stated openly that he now was creating an army of 100,000 men. He traveled throughout the West seeking recruits and money for his venture. He also announced that his enterprise was to be called the Northern Mexico Occupation and Development Company.[69] Although Cutting again sent recruiters to such widespread places as Denver, Austin, and St. Louis, and received a considerable amount of newspaper coverage for his venture, he was never able to raise enough money to get underway. Most people undoubtedly recognized that he was a crackpot unlikely to succeed at anything he tried.[70] The United States government finally warned Cutting and others who might think of filibustering in Mexico that anyone caught implementing such schemes would be fined and imprisoned. Cutting then embarked upon an extended speaking tour of the American South, apparently to win interest and funding. He was unsuccessful, but he did speak loudly of the Monroe Doctrine and of United States expansion into Mexico and Central America. In the early days of 1887, Cutting finally gave up and returned to New Mexico and the newspaper business. Nothing more is known of his filibustering activities.

At least one clue to Cutting's failure can be found in his recruiting techniques. In Denver he or one of his associates ran an advertisement in the local newspaper seeking volunteers for the expedition. One man from Kansas City who was in town and had followed Cutting's activities in the newspapers, went to the recruiting station named in the advertisement and found it to be a saloon. He learned only that a local attorney had used the location to recruit, but that no one knew anything more about the plan. The bartender evidently knew nothing about the expedition, or even that his saloon was the recruiting depot. The man from Kansas City told the local newspaper of his findings. Such revelations disuaded many people from taking the expedition seriously. Matías Romero remarked that "the whole story of this frontier conspiracy is discredited by its grotesque absurdity: by the gross ignorance of the situation in Mexico."[71] Cutting might have failed to realize his expedition, but he had inflamed public opinion on both sides of the border and made life so miserable for Henry R. Jackson, minister to Mexico, that he resigned his position.[72]

News of Cutting's failure scarcely had subsided when rumors prevailed of yet another venture. In early 1889 several men in San Francisco attempted to organize a new expedition. There was considerable substance to these rumors. In fact, the Mexican minister in Washington suggested to the Mexican consul in San Francisco that Mexico was extremely concerned about these rumors and that perhaps the Mexican government should hire a private investigator to look into them. The Mexican secretary of foreign relations agreed to the plan and said that $8 per day plus expenses would not be too exorbitant for the services. It took several weeks to resolve all the details of hiring the detective. During those weeks, more information about the filibuster was revealed in local newspapers and in information sent to the Mexican government from its consuls in the United States. A. K. Coney, Mexican consul in San Francisco, pronounced filibustering a genuine threat "against the integrity of Mexico," and called it "an act of piracy" which hinders "cordial relations between countries."[73]

What was known of this latest filibuster was that unnamed persons had approached members of the Grand Army of the Republic and asked them to join the group. The organizers, among them ex-Confederate Army Colonel J. K. Mulkey, a supposed correspondent for the Louisville, Kentucky, newspaper, claimed they belonged to the "Secret Order of the Golden Field," an old Confederate organization that surfaced in Los Angeles in 1888.[74] The movement concocted a flag with a golden field bearing a St. Andrew's Cross of two red stripes and a single white star in the center, showing some resemblance to the Confederate flag. The plan would have 1500 men posing as farmers and miners leave from Texas, Southern California, and Arizona to invade Baja California. They would become Mexican citizens and six months later start a revolution to create the new republic.[75]

Colonel George W. Gibbons, an ex-Confederate officer and lawyer in New York City, claimed he was actually president of the society and wanted to colonize Baja California and annex it to the United States. Gibbons said the British were moving to gain control of Baja and he planned to beat them to it. Gibbons also claimed he had just met with an Indian aide society in New York City that had given him $2500 and intended to work with Mexicans. The Moravian church allegedly agreed to oversee the missionary efforts. Gibbons also offered that the organization had been organized in 1868 by several ex-Confederate army officers who wanted to see the United States colonize the entire north American continent. The group also may have been comprised of investors in the International Company, a Connecticut-chartered firm that owned large land investments in Baja California and wished to create interest in the property. Moreover, the filibustering effort corresponded with the failure of land speculation in Mexico in which the company had invested heavily. Newspaper sources commented that Gibbons was a "notorious New York lawyer," who was always scheming or promoting in some fashion, but never seemed to carry out anything. The same newspapers speculated that he apparently profited from the planning.[76]

If publicity was what Gibbons wanted, he was getting it. The *New York Herald* of April 17, 1889, reported that 5000 men of a so-called Orden del Terreno de Oro, sometimes referred to as La Liga de Anexión Americana, were poised to enter Baja California. The editor believed that Charles Edward Robinson, who claimed to be an ex-Texas Ranger and Indian fighter and recent real estate broker in Los Angeles, was also involved. Robinson evidently had already sent a few gold seekers into Baja California.[77] Gibbons, when asked about Robinson, admitted that he was a partner in this venture, but that this effort was just a harmless colonization scheme to share in the rich gold mines of Baja California. Whether the scheme was real or dreaming on the part of the entrepreneurs did not matter to Mexicans. They took the matter seriously. The United States tried to show good faith in resolving the filibustering problem and allowed 180 Mexican soldiers armed with modern Remington rifles to travel by train from El Paso to San Diego in order to be in position in Baja California should the filibustering threat materialize.[78]

On April 17, 1889, Mexican authorities in the United States hired Wilkinson and Company of New York City to investigate the rumors. On the same day, Mexicans were again villified in the press. The *New York Daily Tribune* editor wrote that "the border country is full of desperadoes and adventurers who would like nothing better than to attempt to wrest the control of the peninsula from the sparse population, mostly of mongrel Spaniards and Indians now inhabiting it and offer it to the United States."[79] Matías Romero, still in Washington, took notice and advised his government that while such feelings existed in the United States—particularly in California and Texas—there was not enough overall support in the country to threaten Mexico.

On May 27, 1889, after sending an agent to Mexico and California, Wilkinson and Company reported that there was no substance to the rumors. The agency's representative could find no actual filibustering organization, but he did talk to a Frank Adams, an attorney at San Luis Obispo, California, who claimed to be a member of an organization dedicated to annexing both Sonora and Baja California to the United States. Adams claimed that the organization had prominent members in California, Arizona, and New Mexico. Captain J. F. Janes of San Pedro, California (who was later involved in other filibusters), admitted that he was interested in the filibuster, but only to establish an independent country, not to annex the region to the United States. Mexican authorities paid the agency $90 plus expenses for eight days' work, but officials were suspicious about the report.

Mexican skepticism undoubtedly related to articles that had appeared in local California newspapers for years. Captain J. F. Janes had written in his *San Pedro Shipping Gazette* of December 22, 1883, for example, that:

> Lower California we must have: it belongs naturally to Alta California. The peninsula in the hands of the Mexican government is worthless to them, and always will be. Her mountains and canyons are full of wealth, her valleys fertile, and only want American push and capital to show her natural resources. The government of this country must buy it, or we will have to take it for our own protection. Buy it if we can, if not we must take it. I have lived in her and know the country.[80]

Mexicans sincerely believed that the talk of organizing the filibuster was not merely rumor. They also thought that there were prominent Mexicans involved, including Manuel Sánchez Facio, who opposed Porfirio Díaz. Mexicans speculated that Sánchez Facio hoped to use the United States adventurers to help overthrow the Díaz regime.[81] In fact, Sánchez Facio's name surfaced in local newspapers in November 1889 as a possible conspirator. He and others, according to the papers, had met secretly in San Diego to plan a filibustering expedition. Nothing came of the plot, and, for a short time, the rumors subsided.

Many Mexican officials felt that nothing had changed since the 1850s. The United States still tolerated the promotion and organization of illegal expeditions and acted to stop them only when it had become absolutely necessary to preserve good relations with Mexico. Mexicans were also aware of the racist bias Americans held for latinos, and despite the efforts of men such as Matías Romero, hostile sentiment in Mexico increased.

6

1890-1921

I n 1893 Republican William McKinley became president of the United States—a time when expansionists like Theodore Roosevelt wanted to acquire territory in the Caribbean for naval bases. Roosevelt and others had been influenced by Alfred Thayer Mahan's 1890 volume *The Influence of Sea Power on History, 1660-1783*. Mahan argued that the United States needed the presence of a big navy and colonies in or near Latin America as coaling stations for fleet maintenance. Before the 1890s ended the United States demonstrated how imperialistic it could be when it waged war with Spain, forcing Spain to surrender the last of its empire in the Caribbean and in the Pacific. In this period the American government expressed no official interest in acquiring more Mexican territory, although the attitude of expansionism encouraged filibustering and caused renewed concern for Mexico. In the fall of 1914, Mexico's fears were justified when President Woodrow Wilson sent United States troops to occupy Veracruz and in 1916 when troops were deployed in Chihuahua in search of Francisco "Pancho" Villa after the infamous raid on Columbus, New Mexico. Between 1890 and 1921, however, some Americans still dreamed of separating the northern frontier of Mexico from the republic.[1]

Porfirio Díaz, who first gained power in 1872, remained in control of Mexico until 1911. Díaz brought political stability, ultimately controlling Indian raids and discouraging filibusters from entering the country. Under Díaz's leadership Mexico proved its potential for foreign investment. This new revenue brought a measure of modernization. The frontier, however, contin-

ued to lure Americans. Behind some of the activity was United States investment in Mexico and the desire to acquire land and exploit natural resources.

Mexicans were correct in assuming filibustering was not dead, for dur-
ing the early months of 1890 news surfaced in California of another ven-
ture promoted in the name of colonization. Walter G. Smith, editor of the
San Diego Sun and thought to be a personal friend of Vice President Levi
Morton, was said to be the primary organizer. A man calling himself
"Colonel" Edward Hill, a Los Angeles real estate speculator, a "Captain"
Harris, a large land owner in Baja California, Augustus Merrill, editor of
the *San Diego Informant*, described as "a Grand Army Man," B. A.
Stephens, a newspaper manager, and J. K. Mulkey were also allegedly
involved in the scheme. The Mexican Land and Colonization Company,
an English organization that had bought the assets of the International
Company of the United States, was reportedly willing to finance the venture with $100,000.[2]

Evidently this group was aware of Mulkey's efforts to raise a filibustering
expedition and thought they could use his help. Considerable sentiment still
existed in California for a venture into Mexico and it would be easy to get
recruits to join the effort. In April 1889 California newspapers had reported
that Mulkey was organizing, but he vigorously denied the charges.[3] When
Joaquín Díaz Prieto, Mexican consul in Los Angeles, heard of Mulkey's
alleged project, he spoke directly with him. Mulkey denied any knowledge
of such intentions. But Mulkey was involved and schemed with Stephens
and others during 1890. At the time many Californians believed that
Mexicans were so dissatisfied with their government that they would welcome the invaders and a chance to improve their lives. Some miners from
the United States who were working in Baja California were anxious to see
more Americans enter the region also.

B. A. Stephens, who was known widely in California for his views on
annexing Baja California, journeyed from Los Angeles to San Diego in April
1890. On April 7, 1890, Augustus Merrill introduced Stephans to Walter G.
Smith, editor of the *San Diego Sun*, who explained the scheme. The men
agreed to meet again the next evening at the Coronado Hotel. At 8:00 P.M.
the conference, including Merrill, Hill, Smith, and Stephens began. Hill was
the principle spokesman, and he personally pledged $5000 to support the
venture. He claimed to have a friend who would put up an additional

$20,000. The money was all to be refunded from the proceeds of the $100,000 to come from the English company. Hill planned to go to New York City soon, and he would try to find out the cost of guns, ammunition, cannon, and shipping charges from New York. Hill said that a Mr. McQuilter, treasurer of the English company, was ready to commit even more money, but it was recognized that Sir Edward Jenkinson, company president, was hesitant as he had financial interests on the Mexican mainland. Jenkinson realized, however, that if the United States ultimately acquired Baja California, his company assets there would become very valuable. If Jenkinson were aware of the plot he must have been in a quandary.[4]

Hill and Smith had recently journeyed to Ensenada to talk to "Major" Buchanan Scott, who managed the English company's local assets and learned from him that the company might advance a large sum to finance the filibustering effort. Scott suggested that the way to capture the peninsula would include building a railroad to bring American "workers" to Baja California. Before this "immigrant" group arrived, the company's warehouses would be well stocked with guns and supplies. Once the needed arms were in the warehouse and the soldier immigrants in place, Scott would invite all local Mexican officals at Ensenada to a great party at the Hotel Iturbide, a handsome, large and roomy wooden structure on a hill overlooking the port.[5] The Americans would get the Mexicans drunk, bribe the guards at the hotel, and overpower their guests. Scott also told Hill and Smith that he would make available two steamers, the *Manuel Dublán* and the *Carlos Pacheco,* to the filibusters. The Americans returned to San Diego and continued to plot.

Captain J. F. Janes of Los Angeles also arrived in San Diego about this time with the idea of organizing his own expedition. He had written extensively about the value of Baja California and had openly advocated filibustering to accomplish the acquisition. He talked with Smith and Merrill and decided to abandon his own plans and to join their venture. Hill, Smith, and others planned to establish a council of fifteen men who would govern and from whom the officers of the country would be selected.

On Monday evening April 7, 1890, this group held its first formal meeting. One member, who was going to Ensenada soon, was to check on the number and disposition of troops at the Mexican army barracks. Also, he was to see if a large sum of money was available at the Mexican customs house that the filibusters could confiscate. He left shortly after, then returned to San Diego on April 13 and told his fellow conspirators that considerable dissatisfaction existed with the Mexican government. He believed, in fact, that the Mexicans and Americans who lived in Ensenada were ready to see the area annexed to the United States. He added that there was no large sum of money at the customs house.

On April 21, 1890, the conspirators met at the office of the *Informant* and agreed that each would head a department of the new government. In advance, all would prepare a plan of operation for their departments. Two days later they met again at the same location. Walter G. Smith read a declaration of independence of the peninsula and presented his inaugural address that he would give upon assuming his position as president of the New Republic of Baja California. Merrill, who was to become commanding general of the military, shared his plans; Ranford Worthing read an elaborate finance plan, including the details on the printing of money; and B. A. Stephens, secretary general, read the proposed constitution which was to be in effect by August 1, 1890. Others to hold positions in the new government were "Colonel" Edward Hill, a former Civil War general, and C. A. Harris, surveyor general. The positions of attorney general, postal general, and industrial general were as yet unfilled. Local Mexicans supporting the filibusters would occupy those positions.

While the men discussed the details of establishing their republic, they also designed a national flag. It was to have a red field with a small oblong white field next to the pole. The white field would contain a blue star. A narrow orange stripe would extend horizontally from the outer edge of the white field, equidistant from the top and bottom. At the meeting Merrill, in his capacity as military commander, told the group that he had talked with an army officer on leave at Coronado Island. The soldier told him it would take six Napoleon field pieces, several Gatling guns, 1000 Winchester rifles, and many other supplies to hold the peninsula. The men left the last meeting optimistic about their scheme.

Immediately after the meeting Merrill started recruiting his army. On April 26, for some unknown reason, Captain J. F. Janes told a Los Angeles newspaper reporter about the scheme. The story of the impending expedition appeared in a Los Angeles newspaper. On separate occasions Smith and Merrill had journeyed to Los Angeles to see Janes and, in the process, learned that Janes thought the others were making money on the scheme and cutting him out. Unfortunately for the cabal, the Los Angeles paper that published the news learned of the visit of the two officers and more details of the filibustering scheme, then published complete information about the plot. On May 21, 1890, the *San Diego Union*, having picked up the story from the Los Angeles paper, also published details about the plan. On learning that newspapers were aware of their intent, the men involved immediately "took to the brush," as one reporter wrote.[6]

During May 1890, the filibustering scheme became a hot topic for conversation throughout California. United States customs officials in Los Angeles had heard about the plan and had been investigating the rumors for several days. Mexican officials also had repeatedly asked the United States to do something. Americans and Mexicans were aware of the names of the men involved and that their ultimate aim was to annex Baja California to the United States.

On May 22, 1890, Tomás Valdespina Figueroa, Mexican consul in San Diego, reported that Major Scott of the English company was involved and that Scott had been heard to say he would eventually see the British flag fly over Baja California. Others told Valdespina Figueroa that Scott also had said that the peninsula would be better off under United States control if the British could not take command. The Mexican consul's informants told him that everyone was interested in Baja California because it was sparsely settled and said to include many gold and silver deposits ripe for exploitation.[7]

When the story became public knowledge, some of the plotters admitted that they were serious about entering Mexico. Walter G. Smith was confronted by reporters about his part in the scheme, but he claimed that it was only a ruse meant to create a sensation. One reporter for the *San Diego Union* said he had secretly been present at one of the organizational meetings of the group. He maintained that he crawled on his stomach into the room where the meeting was being held, listened and took notes. No one believed his story, most thinking that Janes leaked the details.[8] Who betrayed the filibusters was not as significant as the fact that the betrayal and ensuing publicity ended the venture. It was a serious threat and Mexican officials viewed it so. Other Mexicans believed that it offered an excellent opportunity to stop filibustering once and for all. They suggested that the best thing that could happen was for 200 to 300 filibusters to come to Baja California.

Defenders would be ready for them and after capturing the group would line them up beside the Iturbide Hotel and shoot them.

The rumors of the expedition occasioned the usual outburst of correspondence between Mexican government officials and the United States. General Luis E. Torres, governor and jefe político of Baja California, who had read San Diego newspaper accounts of the filibustering band, wrote to President Porfirio Díaz on May 23 to report what he knew about the filibustering rumors. Torres told Díaz that the United States authorities in San Diego were investigating.[9]

From Washington, Matías Romero reported on the developments of the recent filibustering rumors. He told Ignacio Mariscal, secretary of foreign relations, that he had spoken with James G. Blaine, United States secretary of state, about the continuing problem. Blaine had called him to his office to report that there evidently was a filibustering expedition against Baja California being organized in California. Blaine claimed that the United States was sending troops to the frontier to stop the expedition. The secretary of state also told Romero he did not think the expedition would get underway because the organizers did not have sufficient funding.

Blaine assured Romero that if an expedition were readied to attack Mexico, the United States would arrest the perpetrators and punish them. United States statutes provided for a $3000 fine and a maximum of three years in federal penitentiary for violating the nation's neutrality laws. If the filibusters somehow managed to enter Mexico, Blaine told Romero that the Mexicans should do what they wished with them. Romero responded that he did not think that his countrymen in Baja California would join the filibusters.[10] By this time Romero was convinced that what had been printed in newspapers in California was exaggerated and that much of the story was pure fabrication.[11]

On May 23, 1890, Romero received a long telegram from General Luis Torres detailing the news stories concerning the expedition. Torres made it clear that he was not unduly worried. Torres claimed that he had watched the events carefully, had shown considerable energy in exposing the details of the expedition, and had passed all information to Romero and Díaz.[12] Rumors surfaced at the time that Manuel Sánchez Facio and Manuel Tinoco, both of whom had been functionaries of the Mexican government somewhat earlier, were plotting to assist the group in occupying Baja

California.[13] Mexican secret agents in the United States also heard that Sánchez Facio might be involved, and that ex-governor of Baja California Manuel Castro also favored the venture.[14]

Many Mexicans opposed any type of foreign intervention. Colonel Manuel A. C. Ferrer, an extremely wealthy Mexican who owned a great deal of property in Durango, Sonora, and Baja California, and who had served with the Eleventh Cavalry Regiment of the Mexican Army, was extremely offended not only at the attempted filibustering expeditions, but also at the attitude and pronouncements of some of those involved when they talked about Mexicans. He had read that editor Smith had written that Mexicans were "invincible in peace" and "invisible in war." Ferrer took this as a personal challenge and referred to such talk as "low and base expression." He offered his services and those of 100 armed men—he would recruit, train, and pay them—to the governor of Baja California for use against the *gringos*. He said he would fight Smith alone with "pistols, swords or fists, whatever he may choose, to determine whether a Mexican is a coward, as he has publicly charged."[15]

When Walter G. Smith heard of Ferrer's challenge, he remarked that he was in the editorial offices of his newspaper from 8:00 A.M. until 4:00 P.M. each day and available for the confrontation. Smith also said he believed Ferrer wanted to get him across the border and "then with the usual chivalrous conduct of the Mexicans generally, I would either be shot or stabbed from behind."[16] Smith innocently exclaimed that he was not and had not been involved in the filibustering scheme, except to assist a Colonel Edward Hill of Michigan to obtain information about Mexico.

The fact that the expedition did not succeed did not detract from the damage such activities did to United States-Mexican relations. Much of what was published in the United States was, as it had been for decades, quite inflammatory. Soon after publication the news usually reached the Díaz government in Mexico City. Racial slurs continued. In the May 24, 1890, issue of the *San Diego Republic*, edited by B. A. Stephans, the xenophobic attitudes were clearly visible. Stephans and a co-editor described Baja California as a:

grand peninsula containing 60,000 square miles and with a native population of less than 30,000. Its coast line is indented by some of the grandest harbors in the world. Mexico has ceased to be a republic and is no longer worthy of treatment as such. It is ruled by a bastard Masonic aristocracy headed by dictator Díaz. A majority of its people are a mongrel race— Spanish, Negro and Indian mixed—the indigenous blood predominating, which must, will and always has disappeared with the coming of the Anglo-Saxon. It is manifest destiny that the Mexican race will vanish before the Americans who will eventually take their land. Ten millions of people against seventy millions are only one against seven, and still less when the seven are strong and healthy and the one has quick consumption.

❋ ❋ ❋ ❋ ❋

Even now General [William] Vandever is vigorously pushing through Congress a joint resolution for the purpose of establishing a joint commission with Mexico, for 'readjustment of boundaries.' Is anybody so foolish as to suppose that he stands alone?[17]

Such nonsense obviously had a profound influence on Mexican relations with the United States.

Matías Romero read the articles about Mexico and Mexicans, but again reminded his government that the hands of authorities in the United States were tied because the first amendment of the U.S. Constitution guaranteed freedom of the press. American officials investigated the rumors, Romero reported, but until conspirators actually led an expedition from United States soil into Mexico, they could do nothing. Some Mexicans suggested that the United States could send the perpetrators of plots against Mexico to Mexico for judgement.

Romero and Manuel de Aspíroz understood the constitutional restrictions and recognized that as long as no crime had been committed the United States would not act.[18] Romero also knew that even if plotters were arrested, they would be tried in California and be quickly acquitted. Romero also was aware that lawyers would defend those accused of filibustering for the publicity alone.[19] And, he told his government, their attorneys would make the conspirators look like heroes. Romero explained to his government the recent legislation in the United States Congress that Representative Vendever had introduced, referring to acquisition of Baja California. Romero reported that there was some sentiment in the House of Representatives to try to acquire Baja California, but that there was insufficient support for the idea.[20] In late June 1890, John W. Foster, United States minister in Mexico, wrote Romero of the continuing rumors of filibustering and that he believed that the schemes of 1889 and 1890 were genuine threats. He doubted, however, that the plotters would be successful, and he believed the Mexicans were well prepared to defend themselves. While the filibustering attempt by the San Diego group fell apart in late May 1890, it did not bring an end to rumors. Nor did it quiet Mexican fears of intervention.[21]

Rumors about the filibustering expedition continued during June 1890. Manuel Sánchez Facio and Manuel Tinoco had been planning all that year to organize their own expedition or to join the San Diego cabal. The Mexican consul general in San Francisco, A. K. Coney, wanted to expose all of the filibustering schemes of 1889 and 1890, and he suggested to his government that Mexico hire American investigators to uncover the activities of Sánchez Facio and Tinoco. The consul recommended that one agent be sent to San Diego, one to Castroville, and one to Arizona to investigate rampant rumors of filibustering expeditions and to find out if Sánchez Facio and Tinoco were involved. To encourage his government, Coney sent a statement from A. M. Burnham, who swore that in August 1889 he had met Sánchez Facio in San Francisco. Burnham claimed that Sánchez Facio said he would organize on the false pretense of overthrowing Díaz, but his real aim was to lead 200 men in an invasion of Baja and ultimately to annex it to the United States. Sánchez Facio allegedly told Burnham that a great many Americans were eager to participate, as was Manuel Tinoco. Similar testimony validated charges that Sánchez Facio and Tinoco were actually scheming to lead some sort of filibustering expedition to Mexico.[22]

Matías Romero queried James G. Blaine about the conspirators. Blaine refused to give Romero any information and said that he only knew what he read in the newspapers. He related that he thought the real instigators were a few Englishmen involved in the Mexican Land and Colonization Company of Baja California, and that these men wanted to convert Baja into an English colony. Romero told Blaine that there was no evidence to support such a charge. Blaine amiably responded that he wanted to cooperate and when he received additional information, he would pass it along.[23] Two days later the United States government officially notified Mexico that it would do nothing at the moment to those who allegedly were planning or had planned the expedition.

Mexican officials remained concerned about the activities of Sánchez Facio and Tinoco. In June 1890, the men were telling any Californians who

At left, William McKinley, twenty-fifth president of the United States *(from the collections of the Library of Congress, Washington, D.C.).*

Below, Woodrow Wilson (at far left) and his cabinet *(courtesy Woodrow Wilson House, Washington, D.C.).*

would listen that they had legal rights to land in Mexico. They would organize an expedition to take the property. Before entering Mexico or continuing with planning they decided to present the land claims to Blaine, asking the United States to pressure Mexico into a favorable agreement. They journeyed to Washington and presented the claims to Blaine in the form of sworn affidavits from land owners. The United States government refused to consider the claims seriously.[24]

Toward the end of June 1890, Blaine finally gave Romero a copy of an investigative report into the filibustering scheme. According to the report and what Blaine told Romero, a Mr. Lear of the California Land and Colonization Company was involved, and, in fact, had taken passage on the bark *Manuel Dublán* from Mexico to San Diego to talk with Walter G. Smith, one of the principles in the filibustering plan organized in San Diego. Lear had not talked directly with or about Sánchez Facio and Manuel Tinoco.[25]

The report that the Department of Justice had provided came out of the investigation conducted by E. C. Foster, a special agent the department had sent to California. Foster learned that while the conspiracy was a fact, there had been little support for it, and slight chance that it would be organized.[26] Foster said that the United States marshal at Los Angeles had hired a detective to attend the meetings of the filibusters and that was how word of the plan originally leaked out. The detective learned that the plotters aimed to enter Mexico and start a revolution in concert with the English colonization effort that Scott led in Baja California. There was no evidence that the parent company in London was interested in the plot and no proof that anyone had violated United States neutrality laws. Nor was there any confirmation that any Mexicans were involved, including Sánchez Facio and Manuel Tinoco. On reading the account, Romero was satisfied that it was accurate.[27] Mexican officials in California and in Mexico remained unconvinced, however, that there was no danger from the plot. They believed that Sánchez Facio and Manuel Tinoco, if not the United States itself, had been involved either with Walter G. Smith and his partners or in trying to organize their own expedition.[28] Mexican agents in the United States continued to investigate.

On June 10, 1890, Romero explained again to his superiors the problems he and the United States government faced in dealing with rumors of filibustering expeditions.[29] Romero reminded his countrymen that the laws of the United States presumed an individual innocent until proven guilty, unlike Mexico which followed Roman law that a person was assumed guilty. He added that judges provided the widest defense and the attorneys would make the plotters appear to be heroes and saviors. He recommended that Mexicans await the arrival of adventurers and make a severe example out of them.[30]

By this time it was evident to all involved that a filibustering scheme had been planned.[31] Beginning with the efforts of Walter G. Smith and his backers in San Diego in 1889, it had widened its appeal and ultimately included Sánchez Facio and Manuel Tinoco, whose real goals and activities remain nebulous.[32] With the failure of the filibustering activities in southern California in 1890, a brief respite occurred before deliberations between the two governments over the problem resumed.[33]

Romero and his countrymen did not have long to wait before new rumors surfaced. In July of 1891 Romero and other Mexican officials in the United States learned that a Captain Annett was organizing 200 men in Norfolk, Virgina, to journey to Mexico to help a group of "revolutionaries" against the government. Annett hired a small bark and sailed with his men to Long Island, New York, where he insisted that he was a treasure hunter searching for sunken Spanish galleons.[34] United States authorities investigated the matter briefly and concluded that Annett was more talk than action and that he posed no threat to Mexico. Skeptical Mexican officials could do nothing but wait and watch. Annett evidently decided against going to Mexico, abandoning whatever scheme he had.

For almost four years there was no threat of filibustering. In 1895 warnings arrived in Mexico City, however, that a filibustering expedition was being organized by two men named Friers and Bethune. A. K. Coney, considerably paranoid and ever alert to conspiracies concerning filibustering, advised his government that the two *filibusteros* from San Francisco had purchased a ship, the *Satano*, and were ready to launch an attack on Baja California. Ostensibly the men were heading for Baja California to take possession of land that they claimed to own but had been unable to exploit. The Mexican government believed that the men were actually filibusters who were ultimately after silver and gold.

The *Satano* was anchored in Oakland Creek and the men reportedly were outfitting it with a large assortment of arms. Farfetched rumors prevailed that they would sail first to Hawaii and then to the Canary Islands before going on to Baja California.[35] One California newsman wrote that the men claimed to have documents legitimizing their activity. The editor also said the filibustering ship was an old schooner with four masts and was in such bad condition that even the toughest sailor would be uneasy about sailing anywhere in it. And, he suggested, the men claimed to have information about buried treasure along a creek in Baja California.[36]

Mexicans were sufficiently concerned about the latest threat that they again made a request to the American government to enforce its neutrality laws. In reponse to Mexican pleas, the United States secretary of the treasury sent a note to the collector of customs in San Francisco telling him to keep the party from sailing. One of the leaders, Alfred Barsteau, denied any illegal intention. He said the company of Friers-Bethune bought the land from Hanburg, Garber, and Company, land agents of Ensenada, some years ago and were merely trying to take possession. The arms and ammunition on board were for hunting.[37]

In the midst of the Frier-Bethune matter, a John Breen of San Francisco announced that he would be leading yet another group to a twenty-six-mile-long, ten-mile-wide island 200 miles off the coast of Baja California. He claimed to have purchased the island in 1882 and wanted control. Whether he actually took a group to the island cannot be ascertained, but what is certain is that this caused the diplomatic relationship between the United States and Mexico to deteriorate again. In fact, Richard Olney, U.S. secretary of state, told the Mexican minister in Washington that he regretted that the Breen and Frier-Bethune edisodes had occured but that newspapers in the United States had picked up on the rumors and made more of them than was warranted.[38]

United States officials soon learned that the Ensenada Land Company had no contact with the Frier-Bethune Company for several years. Whether Frier-Bethune really intended to filibuster in Mexico cannot be determined. The great amount of publicity and the rigid stance Mexican authorities had taken against filibustering precluded any such venture.

Correspondence between the two countries continued into 1896, then the matter simply was dropped. Once again, however, a significant amount of controversy between the two countries erupted, keeping matters sensitive for months after the rumors of the expedition had died completely. Mexicans continued to believe that there was considerable difference between the rhetoric United States officials offered and the reality of genuine efforts to stop filibustering. For a few years after 1896 there were no purely American-organized and sponsored attempts to filibuster into Mexico. Occasionally small groups that organized north of the border sought to over-throw Porfirio Díaz. Sentiment for taking over part of Mexico, however, continued to exist in the United States.[39]

In May 1903 rumors surfaced again that Americans were planning a filibustering expedition into northern Mexico. The Mexican consul at Phoenix, Arizona, advised his government that a small group of *gringos* recently had met to plan an expedition.[40] Rumors prevailed that P. H. Hickey, a local wealthy banker, and some of his associates were behind the movement that would attempt to carve out a new republic. The reason for this new venture was that American residents of Cananea were being treated badly by local Mexican authorities.

On June 5, 1903, Manuel de Aspíroz, Mexico's representative in Washington, asked Secretary of State John Hay to investigate. If the rumors proved to be true, Aspíroz demanded that the U.S. stop the filibuster at once. Hay advised Aspíroz on June 22 that he was ordering the United States attorney for the district of Arizona, Frederick S. Nair, to look into the mat-ter and make certain that neutrality laws were not violated.[41] With the help of the federal marshal in the Arizona district, the United States attorney learned that P. H. Hickey spoke fluent Spanish and had business dealings in Mexico. Hickey had commented publicly that the United States should annex northern Mexico.

The Mexican consul in Phoenix, Agustín Piña, had learned of the alleged plot from a blacksmith named F. Velarde who had overheard a conversation between Hickey and others. Velarde was walking down a street and stopped close enough to Hickey and his friends to hear them talk about annexing northern Mexico. One of the Americans, A. F. C. Kirchoff, a Phoenix liquor dealer, stated loudly that conditions for Americans in Mexico had to improve in thirty to sixty days or there would be "hell raised there."[42]

United States authorities interviewed Kirchoff and Hickey, and both denied any involvement in a filibustering scheme. They also denied having said anything about annexing Mexico. Nair investigated Hickey's business dealings and found that Hickey was financially destitute. The bank in which he was supposed to be a partner was closed and Hickey did not even have an office. Nair concluded that if Hickey had said anything about filibustering it was only talk. He had no way to get money to organize the project. The United States advised Mexico of the findings and promised again to enforce United States neutrality laws. Mexicans remained uneasy about filibustering and continued to overreact to rumors. Still, Mexican officials considered filibustering a form of unofficial intervention, and, characteristically, they never really accepted the conclusion that authorities in the United States had offered in respect to Hickey's involvement in filibustering.

Only four years later rumors were rampant again in Mexico and in the American Southwest of yet another attempt to take Mexican territory. On October 28, 1907, Joaquín Díaz Prieto, Mexican consul in San Francisco, advised his superiors that a movement was underway to invade Isla del Tiburón, an island off the coast of northern Sonora. Mexico claimed the island, but had not established control over it because the Seri Indians who inhabited it—according to the Mexicans the Seris were cannibals—had resisted fiercely over many years. Now it was learned that William Mackey-Caldwell, a soldier of fortune from California, would lead an expedition of 150 men to the island and take control.[43]

Shortly after news of this expedition surfaced, American officials learned that Mackey-Caldwell had been arrested in California for writing bad checks. Authorities began a careful search for him during November, 1907, but could not find him. By December it became obvious that Mackey-Caldwell was either out of the country or dead. Men who knew him speculated that he had been eliminated by one of his many enemies. Whatever the plan or the circumstances of Mackey-Caldwell's disappearance, Mexican authorities again reacted strongly.[44]

Political instability and international difficulties had characterized Mexico during much of its history since it gained independence from Spain in 1821. The conditions made the country appear easy prey for any filibuster who wanted to intervene. In 1877, Porfirio Díaz had finally brought stability and economic progress when he assumed power. He ruled the country until 1911. Although his regime was marked by peace and prosperity, he was notorious for his dictatorial methods. Díaz gained control by making regional *caudillos* or *cabecillas* responsible to the central government. He encouraged foreign investment and modernization, and slowly the country progressed. While things improved economically, not all Mexicans shared in the increasing wealth. Those who were poor when Diáz assumed power remained so throughout his regime as he allied with the elites of the Catholic Church, the army, and businesses.

By 1900, despite economic progress, Díaz faced opposition from middle-class elites in the north who faced foreign domination of the economy. They believed that the Díaz government—in promoting foreign investment—had deprived them of their share of the prosperity. In 1910 Díaz announced that he would not seek reelection. He quickly changed his mind, but northern leaders would not accept his decision. The middle-class elites concluded that the only way to remove the old dictator was through armed rebellion. Franciso I. Madero, a well-to-do Coahuilan hacendado, led the revolt when he called for "Effective Suffrage—No Reelection." In 1910 Madero announced that he would run for president. Díaz had Madero arrested. Madero gained his freedom shortly, but fled to the United States where he proclaimed his Plan de San Luis Potosí, calling publicly for the overthrow of Díaz.

By November 1910, the rebellion had begun. Regional *cabecillas* joined in the effort to remove Díaz. Pascual Orozco, Jr., Francisco "Pancho" Villa, Emiliano Zapata, Alvaro Obregón, Plutarco Elías Calles, and Venustiano Carranza joined the revolution. By early 1911 Mexicans throughout the country were fighting to remove Díaz. They succeeded when on May, 21, 1911, Díaz resigned and went into exile. It soon became obvious that those who fought the old dictator could not agree on their goals. Madero assumed the presidency until February 18, 1913, when he was overthrown and assassinated along with his Vice President José María Pino Suárez. On the demise of Madero, General Victoriano Huerta attempted to revive a Díaz-style dictatorship. Revolutionary elites throughout the country opposed this in a continuing armed rebellion. Between the end of Madero's presidency and approximately 1920, the country was torn by continued fighting as the principal leaders vied for control. Not until well after 1920 did the revolutionary fighting slowly wind down. During the period between 1911 and 1921, the war-torn country encouraged various people to take advantage of the chaos.

By 1911, as the revolt against Díaz intensified, it became increasingly more difficult to separate genuine filibustering threats from anti-government forces who wished to invade Mexico and overthrow the government. In at least one instance, an anti-Díaz group included several Americans.[45] Ricardo and Enrique Flores Magón opposed the Díaz regime for many years. In 1901 at San Luis Potosí, Mexico, they founded the Partido Liberal Mexicano, which included U.S sympathizers. The *partido's* purpose was to replace the Díaz regime with one of its own design. Díaz did not act to stifle the movement until 1906, when he outlawed the party and exiled the brothers to the United states. The Flores Magóns went to California and founded a socialist anti-Díaz newspaper, *Regeneración,* that they ultimately used in 1910 and 1911 to help recruit an army.[46]

The brothers Flores Magón could not raise enough Mexican volunteers for their army and resorted to recruiting free-lance American adventurers. The socialist force they assembled was made up of about half *gringos*—a motley group of United States Army deserters, petty thieves, and other opportunists. These often unsavory sorts sought adventure or opportunity to prosper without working much. Like so many of the erstwhile participants in filibustering expeditions these men were mostly dropouts from the American working class.

The Flores Magón brothers chose Baja California as their target. Several people from north of the international border held important positions in the Flores Magón army. Stanley Williams or William Stanley, as he was also known, who allegedly served in the United States Army during the Spanish-American War; adventurer Caryl AP Rhys Pryce; and Jack Mosby, who might have been a deserter from the United States Marines, were all "generals" in the Liberal Army. These adventurers either led or dreamed of leading the Magonista army into Mexico. The Magonistas ultimately attacked and captured Mexicali, Tijuana, and other frontier villages. Pryce and his command consisting of many *norteamericanos* captured Tijuana, and Williams on February 21, 1911, attacked the village of Algodores east of Mexicali with fifty fighters, many of whom were *gringos.*

Newspapers had quoted Pryce, originally from England, as favoring making Baja California independent from the rest of Mexico; even perhaps of making the region a close affiliate of the United States.[47] He did not have that opportunity, however. Soon after he captured Tijuana for the Flores Magón movement, internal dissension broke out among Pryce's staff. Pryce and his aide crossed into the United States on May 18, 1911, presumably to talk with Ricardo Flores Magón. United States Army troopers arrested them and charged them with violating neutrality laws.[48] They were held for a few days and then released.[49] Before Pryce could reestablish complete control over his forces in and near Tijuana, more dissension surfaced. By June 2, rumors prevailed along the frontier that Pryce had decided to convert his group into a full-fledged filibustering expedition. He never did.[50] One paper reported that "Pryce speaks modestly, but the dream of empire is in his eyes. It is empire for the common man, as he tells it. He stands on the revolutionary manifesto of Ricardo Magon [sic]...." He would establish "a model state with the most advanced institutions. Such a state could live under a liberal regime in Mexico, or as a separate republic, or as part of the United States."[51] Although Pryce had little chance of converting his efforts into an American filibustering effort, Mexico blamed the United States for not stopping the venture.[52] Mexican authorities considered the Flores Magón invasion and the organization of other anti-government movements as filibustering efforts.

Newspaper editors speculated about Pryce and other *gringos* leading expeditions into Mexico.[53] Filibustering rumors had surfaced in February 1911, when Richard Wells Ferris, a promoter and sometime actor in his forties from Los Angeles seeking publicity for himself, allegedly contacted Porfirio Díaz and offered to buy Baja California. Díaz did not respond. Ferris then announced that he would acquire Baja California by conquest if necessary, and that he would be "elected" president of the new country. Continuing his charade, Ferris declared that he would appoint Pryce commander of his army if he could convince Pryce to take the position. Ferris commissioned the design of a flag for the new republic, a country that he said he would name La República de Díaz if Díaz cooperated. If not he would consider naming it the United Republic of Lower California or the Madero Republic of Lower California. Ferris also said that he had the support of monied men in California: "Diamond Field" Jack Davis and Robert Cords, Jr., were going to put up most of the money. Ferris announced that the attack on Baja California would be a "legitimate conquest for the cause of civilization."[54] In May 1911, before Pryce returned to the United States, Ferris journeyed to Tijuana where Pryce had established his headquarters and talked with him about a cooperative venture in Baja California. Soon thereafter Pryce, who had become disillusioned with the Magonistas, crossed into the United States to resolve conflicts with Flores Magón. Pryce did not to return to command of the forces. In late May a member of Pryce's group, Louis James, decided to convert Pryce's forces into a filibustering expedition. At this point Ferris returned to

Tijuana and talked with James, encouraging him to act independently of the Flores Magón movement. Ferris then headed to San Diego. He soon heard from James, who told him that Ferris had been elected president of the new republic, and he should come at once to Tijuana. Ferris declined.

For good reason American newsmen and authorities did not take Ferris seriously.[55] The newspapers always looked for some story to help sell papers, and the local editors knew that Ferris was primarily a clown. Although people in the United States did not take him seriously, many Mexicans did and asked that the United States put an immediate stop to this filibustering effort.[56] Ferris apparently decided that his charade had gone too far. On June 3, with newspaper reporters asking questions and United States authorities watching closely, Ferris announced that he had not been involved in the venture and that his election to the presidency of Baja California had been without his consent. Jack Mosby, who took Pryce's place as commander of the Flores Magón forces, announced that Ferris had never had anything to do with the efforts of the Liberal Party in Mexico.

The Flores Magón rebellion was anti-government and had no connection with Ferris. Ferris may have been a fool seeking self-promotion and in that vein he succeeded. There might not have been any chance that he or others could have created a filibustering expedition out of the Flores Magón activities, but the significance of the rumors was to affect Mexican official and public opinion. Yet again, in the eyes of Mexicans, Americans who believed that opportunity existed south of the border had tried to use internal difficulties in Mexico to establish a foothold on their territory. More significantly, the Mexican government claimed that the United States had been behind the movement, hoping to grab Baja California. The Americans had stationed large numbers of troops along the international border with Baja California, and to Mexicans this appeared to be preparation to intervene when the opportunity arose.

Among those who stood to lose land and influence in northern Mexico if the revolution swept across Baja California and land was redistributed to peasants were Harrison Gray Otis and his son-in-law Harry Chandler, both wealthy California newspapermen.[57] During and immediately after 1914, Otis and Chandler might have been involved in a filibustering conspiracy. They owned the California-Mexico Land and Cattle Company, the Mexican chartered subsidiary of the Colorado River Land Company, a vast enterprise with several million acres in Baja California. They had purchased the land from General Guillermo Andrade in 1900 but had done little to develop it. As the Mexican revolution raged through 1915, Otis and Chandler may have schemed with Baltázar Avilés, ex-governor of Baja California (who had been forced to leave his position in 1914 by Estéban Cantú), and several others to protect their investments. The Mexican government considered this another of the continuing filibustering attempts organized in the United States. Ultimately, the United States government acted to stop this new scheme before it could be put into motion by bringing charges against the men for violation of neutrality acts. According to official charges, the men hired Manuel Brassell and J. N. Fernández to establish a base of operations at El Centro, California, where they would stockpile munitions and supplies in preparation for entering Mexico. Avilés was to be the primary organizer, but he allegedly received financing from Otis and Chandler.

Early in 1915 the United States brought indictments against the conspirators for violation of neutrality laws, but attorneys for Chandler and Otis stalled for time, delaying the case until 1917 when charges were dropped. The presiding judge decreed that the case was not strong enough to proceed, and he believed that the defense attorneys clearly had discredited the government's witnesses. Mexicans, however, did not accept the ruling, thinking that it was yet another attempt on the part of the United States to support and cover up intervention. There was never any solid evidence, in fact, that Chandler and Otis had been involved.[58]

Rumors continued about armed intervention in Baja California. Estéban Cantú, governor of the northern district of Baja California from 1915 to 1921 who was opposed to United States influence in Mexico, may have given rise to some of the rumors by encouraging an ex-United States Army captain named Dineley (or Dingley) to intercede. Cantú was angry about the Constitutionalist government's execution of fourteen of his associates, including General Pedro González. He wanted revenge. During his reign on the frontier Cantú frequently did not support the central government; he was more interested in perpetuating his power. Cantú might have considered a separatist movement in Baja California, but not with the idea of annexing Baja to the United States. Mexican officials accused Cantú of such a movement and tried to discredit him by branding him as an operator of a bawdy house (which was true), and a man of questionable character. The Mexican government believed that Dineley was a gun-runner who saw Cantú's dissatisfaction as an opportunity to organize. If involved, Cantú undoubtedly believed that Dineley could be of use. According to some sources, Dineley planned to attack Mexicali and Tijuana. His men would drive Ford school buses loaded with well-armed filibusters across the border.[59]

Dineley claimed he was an agent of the Auto-Ordinance Corporation and that he had been paid to take 150 Thompson sub-machine guns to Baja California. He denied that he would use the guns to attack a Mexican outpost. He admitted that he would, however, be accompanied by approximately 200 men. The Mexican army had only 600 poorly trained, poorly armed, and poorly disciplined men stationed near Tijuana. Mexican authorities learned of the shady activities from a deserter from the group who also told them that the invading party would use an airplane to destroy Mexican coastal fortifications.[60] There was additional speculation on both sides of the border that the movement involved leading United States politicians, including Senators Albert B. Fall of New Mexico and Henry F. Ashurst of Arizona. In fact, Fall had for a long time been outspoken on behalf of intervention in Mexico.

In the closing months of 1919 and early in 1920 Fall conducted Senate hearings concerning Mexico and pressured Woodrow Wilson to intervene in Mexican internal affairs, particularly after some of the nationalistic aspects of the Constitution of 1917 were being implemented. Fall was angry at Mexico; he had lost money investing in mines in Chihuahua during 1912. Fall was not alone among United States officials interested in Mexico. Senator Ashurst began discussion of the Mexican question by introducing in January 1919 a Senate resolution calling for the purchase of Lower California and a tract of land in Sonora. Ashurst found support for this proposal from Democrats also. Senator William H. King of Utah agreed that the United States should acquire Baja California.[61] Though acting on his own and for fellow investors, Mexicans viewed Fall as an official of the United States and his actions as representative of United States policy.

Others in Mexico thought this could be a movement by the *científicos* of Díaz's inner circle who supported modernization, foreign invesment and their reactionary supporters.[62] It was not unusual for prominent Mexicans to refuse to support the government between 1890 and 1920. Luis Cabrera, Pedro González, Francisco Murguía and many others who supported Venustiano Carranza from 1913 to 1920 refused to support the government of Alvaro Obregón, who was elected in 1920.

If filibusters invaded Baja California, Mexican general Abelardo L. Rodríquez, stationed at Mexicali, was confident he could drive them out. He did not believe, however, that an invasion would happen.[63] United States authorities again advised the Mexican government that they would do all possible to stop any illegal *entradas* into Mexico. In mid- October 1921, the government related to the Mexican authorities that American agents had just captured three trucks four miles north of the border loaded with guns and ammunition. The trucks, heading for Mexico, contained 250 rifles, 80,000 cartridges, and other explosives. According to unsubstantiated reports, the ordnance was to be delivered to Luis Parma, who lived near the border.[64] In addition, a reporter for the *San Diego Sun* wrote that he had just learned that Cantú had organized 150 men in San Diego early in November with the aim of securing control of all of Baja California. The men were to be paid $1.50 per day and expected to conduct themselves as soldiers.[65] In San Diego, county authorities responded to the news by arresting and disarming the volunteers. The men were detained a short while and then told to get out of town.[66]

Leadership and membership in this group was wider than many United States officials realized. It might have been that Luis Parma of Nester, California, who lived just five miles from Tijuana, was a paymaster for the group. Felipe Verdugo could have been second-in-command, and Lerdo González the chief military leader. About thirty volunteers were receiving pay and the group met regularly at the Pacific Hotel or Pete's Place in San Diego. Mexican officials speculated that there were several of these groups but they were not all working together. There might have been 200 to 300 men involved. Some were well armed, and rumors prevailed that one cabal had two airplanes. The principal group, however, probably had its head-quarters in Los Angeles.[67] Cantú's relationship in the activity cannot be ascertained. One group of armed Mexicans and United States citizens entered Mexico in November 1921, and advanced forty miles south of Tijuana when Colonel Anselmo Armenta and 200 Mexican troops, depart-ing from Tijuana on November 15, confronted them. In the fight that ensued, the Mexican Army killed nine of the intruders and captured twenty more. They also captured 275 rifles, a large number of Thompson sub-machine guns, and other weapons and ammunition.[68]

A short time afterward, another party crossed into Mexico six miles from

Tijuana to avoid the Mexican troops. This party did not remain in Mexico long. After marching around the area for a day, the group returned to American soil. When they entered the United States, immigration authorities arrested them and turned them over to the Department of Justice. Mexican officials, on learning of the party, charged once again that the United States was guilty of bad faith for not stopping the activity before it occurred. In fact, the Mexicans believed that at least one member of the Department of Justice was running guns across the border to help the United States obtain Baja California.[69]

The purpose, composition, and specific activities of filibustering groups hoping to enter Mexico in 1921 remains unclear.[70] What is fairly certain is that many people in the United States, almost seventy-five years after the acquisition of a considerable amount of Mexican territory, still cast covetous eyes upon northern Mexico, particularly Baja California, and sought to take advantage. Suggestions that the United States pressure Mexico to sell the entire peninsula were rampant at that time and have surfaced from time to time even to the present. In 1938 the *San Diego Union* contained an Associated Press dispatch from Oklahoma City stating that an oil man urged the purchase of Baja California. W. E. Ramsey, who had moved from Oklahoma to Los Angeles, wrote Oklahoma Senator Elmer Thomas suggesting that the United States buy the area for $500,000,000 so Mexico could have money to pay Americans for losses in the recent expropriation of oil-company property. The rest of the money could be used to build railroads for Mexico. Even in more recent times United States politicians have remarked that the United States should try to purchase Baja California.

7

CONCLUSION

Throughout the history of U. S.-Mexican relations, Mexicans have believed that *gringo* involvement in filibustering groups that violated Mexican territory was a form of state-sponsored intervention that threatened the country's sovereignty. On many occasions in the past Mexican officials have said as much publicly. U.S. authorities have not taken Mexico's complaints seriously and, in fact, have stated that some of these were based solely on rumors of violations of Mexican territory. Even if U. S. officials believed there were any substance to the rumors, they did not think any group organizing north of the international border posed a significant threat to Mexico.

Border problems during the last half of the nineteenth and first two decades of the twentieth century were in some respects similar to contemporary problems although in reverse. The difficulties today focus upon myriad items, but to many groups in the U.S. the flow of illegal drugs and undocumented migrants possibly threaten U.S. national security, if not its sovereignty. During the period included in this study Mexico believed that the U.S. was not doing what it could to stop schemers and dreamers from violating its borders. It is worthwhile, however, to consider that the border is 2000 miles long and is very permeable. During the period of this study, the U.S. repeatedly advised Mexico that it could not stop the violations completely. In fact, during a considerable period of the nineteenth century the U.S. did not effectively control its own American West in respect to banditry, Indian raids, and general lawlessness. Political and economic problems contributed to this failure. For example, within a few years of the end of the Civil War, the strength of the U.S. Army was limited to 25,000 men, a number far too small to police the western half of the country. It was after 1890 before the U.S. resolved its security problems in the West. Even if the U.S. had sincerely wanted to stop the groups planning to enter Mexico during the nineteenth century, it is doubtful the forces available could do so.

Trans-border problems today, at least for Mexico, are not much different from what they were for the U.S. during the years included in this study. The U.S. complains to Mexico about illegal traffic crossing the border and blames Mexico for not cooperating fully in controlling the southern side of the international boundary. The border problems today, however, are for Mexico somewhat similar to what they were for the U.S. in the past. While the border is more populated now, there remain thousands of miles of scarcely populated or deserted trans-border territory that cannot be policed either by the Mexican forces or those of the U.S. Mexico, like the U.S. in the nineteenth century, does not have the forces to stop illegal drugs and immigration from entering the U.S. Political and economic problems plague Mexico today just as they did the U.S. in the earlier period. One additional factor is important for understanding the trans-border problems both historically and today. Clearly in the nineteenth century there was considerable popular support in the U.S. for acquiring more Mexican territory. U.S. citizens also were sympathetic to any group wishing to enter Mexico and straighten out what some people in the U.S. considered a political, social, and economic disaster south of the line. Today there is sympathy in Mexico for those individuals who want to migrate in any fashion to the U.S. to find work to support their families. Finally, Mexicans point to the U.S. demand for drugs as the reason for the problem. Border difficulties in some regards have come full circle since 1848: if modern-day conflicts are to be understood, individuals on both sides must place the problems within the context of trans-national history.

NOTES

PREFACE

1. Angela Moyano Pahissa, *México y Estados Unidos: Orígenes de una relación, 1819-1861* (México, D.F.: Secretaría de Educación Pública, 1985); Luis G. Zorilla, *Historia de las relaciones entre México y Estados Unidos de América, 1800-1958*, 2 tomos (México, D.F.: Editorial Porrúa, 1965).
2. Josefina Zoraida Vásquez and Lorenzo Meyer, *The United States and Mexico* (Chicago: The University of Chicago Press, 1985), 2.
3. *Ibid.,* 54-55.
4. *Ibid.,* 55.
5. Vásquez and Meyer, *The United States and Mexico*, 62.
6. Patrick Oster, *The Mexicans: A Personal Portrait of a People* (New York: William Morrow and Co., 1989), 101, 126.
7. John H. Coatsworth and Carlos Rico (eds.), *Images of Mexico in the United States* (San Diego: Center for U.S.-Mexican Studies, 1989), 1.
8. See W. Dirk Raat, *Revoltosos: Mexico's Rebels in the United States, 1903-1923* (College Station: Texas A&M University Press, 1981); Ward S. Albro, *Always A Rebel: Ricardo Flores Magón and the Mexican Revolution* (Fort Worth: Texas Christian University Press, 1992); Lowell L. Blaisdell, *The Desert Revolution, Baja Califorina, 1911* (Madison: The University of Wisconsin Press, 1962); Don M. Coerver and Linda B. Hall, *Texas and the Mexican Revolution: A Study in State and National Border Policy, 1910-1920* (San Antonio: Trinity University Press, 1984); Linda B. Hall and Don M. Coerver, *Revolution on the Border: The United States and Mexico, 1910-1920*

(Albuquerque: University of New Mexico Press, 1988) and William O. Scroggs, *Filibusters and Financiers, William Walker and His Associates* (New York: The MacMillan Co., 1916).

1: ANTECEDENTS

1. A work that covers this early background is Charles H. Brown, *Agents of Manifest Destiny: The Lives and Times of the Filibusters* (Chapel Hill: University of North Carolina, 1980). This book does not detail all filibustering into Mexico, rather it focuses on Narciso López's expeditions to Cuba and William Walker's to Nicaragua. Information concerning filibustering into Baja California is treated briefly. See also, Scroggs, *Filibusters and Financiers*, Lawrence Greene, *The Filibuster, The Career of William Walker* (Indianapolis: The Bobbs-Merrill Co., 1937), and Gastón García Cantú, *Invasiones norteamericanas en México* (México, D.F.: Serie Popular Era, 1971).
2. Julius W. Pratt, *Expansionists of 1812* (New York: The Macmillan Co., 1925), 371-374.
3. *Ibid.,* 88.
4. Francisco de Arrangoiz, Mexican consul at New Orleans, to Secretaría de Relaciones Exteriores, May 27, 1844, in "Francisco Sentmanat, Intercambio de Correspondencia entre México—Nueva Orleans sobre la Expedición de Francisco Sentmanat y su Fusilamiento en Tabasco," Fil-3-(I), 10, Archivo Histórico Genaro Estrada de la Secretaría de Relaciones Exteriores, México. Hereafter, cited as AHSRE.
5. Arrangoiz, "Sentmanat, July 11, 1844, 18.
6. See Paul F. Lambert, *The All Mexico Movement* in Odie B. Faulk and Joseph A. Stout, Jr., eds., *The Mexican War: Changing Interpretations* (Chicago: Swallow Press,1973). See also, Frederick Merk, *Manifest Destiny and Mission in American History* (New York: Alfred Knopf, 1963); John D. Fuller, *The Movement for the Acquisition of All Mexico* (Baltimore: Johns Hopkins Press, 1936); and Albert K. Weinberg, *Manifest Destiny* (Baltimore: Johns Hopkins Press, 1935). A recent work on the U.S.-Mexican War is Richard V. Francaviglia and Douglas W. Richmond, *Dueling Eagles: Reinterpreting the U.S.-Mexican War, 1846-1848* (Fort Worth: Texas Christian University Press, 2000).

2: 1848-1860

1. Ambrose H. Sevier and Nathan Clifford to James Buchanan, Querétaro, May 25, 1848, House Exec. Doc. 50, 30th Cong., 2nd Sess., Serial 541, 74-76. For continuing difficulties comcerning the U.S.-Mexico boundary, see Harry P. Hewitt and Robert Cunningham, "'A Lovely Land Full of Roses and Thorns': Emil Landberg and Mexico, 1835-1866," *Southwestern Historical Quarterly*, vol. 93 (January 1995), 386-425; Herry P. Hewitt, "'El deseo de cubrir el honor nacional': Francisco Jiménez and the Survey of the Mexico-United States Boundary, 1849-1857," in *Ciudad y campo en la historia de México*, Ricardo Sánchez, Eric Van Young and Gisela Von Wobeser, eds., 2 vols. (México, D.F.: Instituto de Investigaciones Históricas, Universidad Nacional Autónoma de México, 1992), 1771-196; Harry P. Hewitt, "The Mexican Boundary Survey Team: Pedro García Conde in California," *Western Historical Quarterly*, vol. 21 (May 1990), 171-196; Harry P. Hewitt, "The Mexican Commission and Its Survey of the Rio Grand Boundary, 1850-1854," *Southwestern Historical Quarterly*, vol. 94 (April 1991), 555-580.

2. The treaty and its implications for Mexico are discussed in Luis G. Zorrilla, *História de las relaciones entre México y los Estados Unidos*, 29, 213-234.

3. Coerver and Hall, *Texas and the Mexican Revolution*, 19.

4. The best general source for this period is Daniel Cosío Villegas, *Historia moderna de México*, 7 tomos (México, D.F.: Editorial Hermes, 1955-1965). There are numerous other sources that deal with either the early or later nineteenth century. See, Wilfred H. Calcott, *Liberalism in Mexico, 1857-1929* (Palo Alto: Stanford University Press, 1931). For the effect of the period on the frontier of Mexico, see Hubert Howe Bancroft, *History of the North Mexican States and Texas,* 2 vols. (San Francisco: The History Co., 1886).

5. William A. Depalo, *The Mexican National Army, 1822-1852* (College Station: Texas A&M University Press, 1997), 139-140, 158-159; see also Pedro Santoni, *Mexicans at Arms: Puro Federalists and the Politics of War, 1845-1848* (Fort Worth: Texas Christian University Press, 1996).

6. See, for example, Walter V. Scholes, *Mexican Politics During the Juárez Regime, 1855-1872* (Columbia: University of Missouri Press, 1957); Justo Sierra, *Juárez su obra y su tiempo* (México, D.F.: Editorial Porrúa, 1905, reprinted, 1970).

7. For specifics about conditions on the frontier of Mexico see, Oscar J. Martínez, *Border Boom Town: Ciudad Juárez since 1848* (Austin: University of Texas Press, 1978); Pablo Martínez, *A History of Lower California* (México, D.F.: Editorial Baja California, 1960); Robert C. Stevens, "Forsaken Frontier: A History of Sonora, Mexico," unpublished Ph.D. dissertation, University of California, 1963; Rodolfo Acuña, *Sonoran Strongman: Ignacio Pesqueira and His Times* (Tucson: University of Arizona Press, 1974); Fernando Jordan, *Crónica de un país bárbaro* (Chihuahua: Centro Librero La Prensa, 1956); Enrique Gonzáles Flores, *Chihuahua de la independencia a la revolución* (México, D.F.: Ediciones Botas-México, 1949); Juan Antonio Ruibal Corella, *Perfiles de un patriota: La huella del general Pesqueira García en el Noreste de México* (México, D.F.: Editorial Porrúa, 1979); Informe de la comisión Pesquisidora de la frontera del norte al ejecutivo de la unión cumplimiento del artículo 3 de la ley de 30 de Septiembre de 1872 (Monterrey, Mexico), Mayo 15 de 1872 (Published México, D.F., Imprenta de Díaz de León y White, 1874); Alberto Calzadíaz Barrera, *Dos gigantes: Sonora y Chihuahua*, 2 tomos, revised edition (Hermosillo: Escritores Asociados del Norte, 1960); José Fuentes Mares, *Y México se refugio en el desierto* (México, D.F.: Editorial Jus, 1954). A general work that surveys the overall border history, although without notes is Thomas Torrans, *Forging the Tortilla Curtain: Cultural Drift and Change along the United States-Mexico Border From the Spanish Era to the Present* (Fort Worth: Texas Christian University Press, 2000).

8. *Colonias militares, proyecto para su establecimiento en las fronteras de oriente y occidente* (México, D.F.: 1848). Copies of this document can be found in numerous places in Mexican archives. For a translated and edited version see, Odie B. Faulk, ed., "Projected Mexican Military Colonies for the Borderlands, 1848," *Journal of Arizona History*, 10 (Spring 1968), 39-47.

9. Mariano Paredes, *Proyectos de leyes sobre colonización y comercio en el estado de Sonora, presentados a la camára de diputados por el representante de aquel estado en la sesión extraordinario del día 1850* (México, D.F.: 1850). Copies are in various Mexican archives. For a translated and edited version see, Odie B. Faulk, ed., "A Colonization Plan for Northern Sonora, 1850," *New Mexico Historical Review*, 44 (October 1969), 293-314.

10. Juan N. Almonte, *Proyectos de leyes sobre colonización* (México, D.F.: 1852). Copies can be found in various Mexican archives.

11. Milo M. Quaife, ed., *James K. Polk, The Diary of James K. Polk During His Presidency, 1845-1849*, 4 vols. (Chicago: A. C. McClurg Co., 1910).

12. For general information see, Jesse S. Reeves, *American Diplomacy Under Tyler and Polk* (Baltimore: Johns Hopkins University Press, 1907); J. Fred Rippy, *The United States and Mexico* (New York: Alfred A. Knopf, 1926); Howard F. Cline, *The United States and Mexico* (Cambridge: Harvard University Press, 1965).

13. Paul N. Garber, *The Gadsden Treaty* (Philadelphia: University of Pennsylvania Press, 1923).

14. For information concerning Buchanan see, John B. Moore, ed., *The Works of James Buchanan*, 12 vols. (New York: Antiquarian Press, 1908-1911). For an overview of this period see, Clarence C. Clendenen, *Blood on The Border: The United States Army and the Mexican Irregulars* (New York: The Macmillan Co., 1969); Oscar J. Martínez, *Troublesome Border* (Tucson: University of Arizona Press, 1988). For a Mexican view of diplomacy see, Angela Moyano Pahissa, *México y Estados Unidos*.

3: 1848-1855

1. Some early filibusters are included in, Joseph A. Stout, Jr., *The Liberators: Filibustering Expeditions into Mexico, 1848-1862, and the Last Thrust of Manifest Destiny* (Los Angeles: Westernlorc Press, 1973). Other aspects of filibustering are detailed in Moyano Pahissa, *California y sus relaciones con Baja California* (México, D.F.: Fondo de Cultura Económica, 1983); Beatríz Eugenia Zamarano Navarro, "Filibusteros Norteamericanas en México (1850-1860)," unpublished thesis, Universidad Nacional Autónoma de México, 1987; and Alejandro Campo Lamas, Catálogo de la serie filibusterismo del Archivo Histórico Genero Estrada (1835-1854)," unpublished thesis, Universidad Nacional Autónoma de México, 1996.

2. See Service File of Joseph C. Morehead, Records of the Adjutant General's Office, RG 94, National Archives and Records Service. See also, *The War of the Rebellion: A Compilation of the Offical Records of the Union and Confederate Armies*, 128 vols. (Washington, D.C.: 1880-1901), series II, IV, 354-355, 702, and series II, VI, 63, for general information about Morehead. The Morehead family never admitted that there was a member named Joseph. In the file cited, Morehead told Joseph E. Johnston, commanding the

Confederate Army, and President Jefferson Davis, that he was the son of ex-governor James Turner Morehead of Kentucky. Morehead tried to get a commission to lead a group of rangers behind Union lines in Kentucky.

3. *Daily Alta California,* January 14, 1851.

4. *Ibid.,* January 8, 18, 1851.

5. The California state legislature investigated Morehead's activities. See, *Journals of the Legislature of California* (Sacramento, 1851), 104-105, 277, 452-479, 496-497. See also, *Daily Alta California,* April 27, 1851.

6. *Daily Alta California,* May 17, and June 3, 1851.

7. *El Sonorense* (Ures), May 30, 1851, Alphonse Pinart Collection, University of California, Berkeley, IV, 312. Hereafter cited as Pinart Collection.

8. Rafael Espinosa to SRE, La Paz, April 19, 1851, in "General José E. Morehead. Filibusteros norteamericanas al mando de Gral. José E. Morehead se dirigen a la península de la Baja California a insurrecionarla para anexarla a los E.U.A," Fil-6-(I), 1-3, AHSRE.

9. *Daily Alta California,* May 24, 1851; *El Sonorense,* August 8, 1851, Pinart Collection, IV, 239.

10. *Daily Alta California,* June 21, 1851.

11. Biographical information can be found in Ernest C. Shearer, "The Carvajal Disturbances," *Southwestern Historical Quarterly,* 55 (October 1951), 201-230.

12. Newspaper clipping, n.d., in Luis De La Rosa, Legación Mejicana en Estados Unidos, to SRE, Washington, October 23, 1851, in Fil-7-(I), AHSRE.

13. Ventura de Alcalá, Consul at Brownsville, Texas, to SRE, October 13, 1851, 10-11, *Ibid.* Mexico was concerned that Carvajal intended to establish a República de la Sierra Madre. See De La Rosa, México, D.F., to Daniel Webster, November 13, 1851, in William R. Manning, ed., *Diplomatic Correspondence of the United States, Inter-American Affairs, 1831-1860,* 12 vols., Washington, 1932-1939, vol. 9, 427.

14. Luis De La Rosa, Washington, to SRE, October 13, 1851, Fil-7-(I), AHSRE, 49-52.

15. Buckingham Smith, México, D.F., to Sec. of State, November 21, 1851, United States Department of State, Dispatches from U.S. Ministers to Mexico, 1823-1926, vol.15, roll 16, RG 59, National Archives. Microfilm

copy Oklahoma State University Library. Hereafter cited as RG 59.

16. Robert P. Letcher, México, D.F., to SRE, México, October 25, 1851, Fil-7-(I), AHSRE, 48-49.

17. Luis De La Rosa, Washington, to SRE, November 15, 1851, *Ibid.*, 106-107.

18. Robert P. Letcher, México, D.F.,to SRE, November 18, 1851, *Ibid.*, 142.

19. José F. Ramírez, México, D.F., to Letcher, January 28, 1852, *Ibid.*

20. *Ibid.*, December 10, 1851, 151.

21. *Río Bravo* (Brownsville, Texas), February 4, 1852, in Fil-7-(VIII), *Ibid.*, 237-239.

22. *La Bandera Americana* (Brownsville, Texas), December 13, 1851, in Fil-7- (II), *Ibid.*, 125.

23. *Río Bravo*, October 31, 1851, *Ibid.*, 106.

24. *El Constitucional Periódico Oficial*, March 6, 1852, *Ibid.*, 177-178.

25. *La Bandera Americana*, December 13, 1851, *Ibid.*, 126.

26. José M. González de la Vega, Legación Mexicana, Washington, to SRE, April 24, 1852, Fil-5-(V), *Ibid.*, 119; see also, *New Orleans Daily Picayune*, May 20, 1852, also in Fil-5-(V), *Ibid.*, 28-29.

27. [?] Robles, México, D.F., to SRE, January 28, 1852, Fil-7-(II), *Ibid.*, 174-175.

28. Information can be found in newspaper clippings with no date, place, or name in Fil-7-(VI), *Ibid.*, 108. See also, Joaquín de Castillo, Brownsville, to SRE, December 10, 1852, Fil-7-(V), *Ibid.*, 153.

29. Manuel Larrainzar, Washington, to SRE, June 16, 1852, *Ibid.*, 48-49; see warning of filibustering from A. García, Monterrey, to SRE, June 27, 1852, in LE-1096, Tomo XLII, *Ibid.*, 32.

30. José Fernando Ramírez, México, D.F., to Robert P. Letcher, July 11, 1852, *Ibid.*, 83-84.

31. Robert P. Letcher, México, D.F., to Ramírez, July 6, 1852, *Ibid.*

32. R. P. Letcher, México, D.F., to Daniel Webster, June 23, 1852, vol .15, roll 16, RG-59.

33. Joaquín J. de Castillo, Brownsville, to SRE, December 10, 1852, LE-1096, Tomo XLII, 153, AHSRE.

34. *Ibid.*, Brownsville, January 31, 1853, Fil-7-(VI), 9, AHSRE.

35. *Ibid.*, Brownsville, April 30, 1853, 65-66.

36. Conkling, México, D.F., to William L. Marcy, Sec. of State, May 5, 1853, vol. 18, roll 19, RG 59.

37. Conkling, México, D.F., to Alamán, May 5, 1853, *Ibid.*
38. See various newspaper clippings, no name, place, or date *Ibid.*, 108.
39. Joaquín J. de Castillo, Brownsville, to SRE, February 15, 1854, Fil-7-(VII), 10, AHSRE.
40. *Ibid.*, Brownsville, August 8, 1854, 93-94.
41. *Ibid.*, August 10, 1854.
42. William L. Marcy, Washington, to Juan N. Almonte, envoy extraordinary and minister plenipotentiary to the U.S., January 10, 1855, Fil-7-(VIII), *Ibid.*, 2-7.
43. *Daily Alta California*, August 15, October 5, 1852.
44. Charles de Lambertie, *Le drame de la Sonora, l'etat de Sonora, M. Le Comte De Raousset Boulbon et M. Charles De Pindray* (Paris: Chez Ledoyen, Libraire Editeur 1855), 208-209; see also, Horacio Sobarzo *Crónica de la aventura de Raousset-Boulbon en Sonora* (México, D.F.: Librería de Manuel Porrúa, 1954), 4; Farrell Symons, tr., *The Wolf Cub: The Great Adventure of Count de Raousset-Boulbon in California and Sonora, 1850-1854,* by Maurice Soulie (Indianapolis: Bobbs-Merril Co., 1927), 80-89. The best work on the French activities in Sonora during this period remains Rufus K. Wyllys, *The French in Sonora* (Berkeley: University of California Press, 1932).
45. Lambertie, *Le drame de la Sonora,* 207-209, and chapter two in its entirety. Materials on the Raousset expeditions are scattered in the AHSRE collections. Some documents are in L-E-1096, others catalogue under the Fil-5-(1-9) numbers. The files contain hundreds of pages on Raousset and this is the largest file in the collection.
46. *New York Daily Times,* June 30, 1852.
47. *El Sonorense,* February 4, 1853; see also, Bancroft, *North Mexican States,* vol. 2, 676.
48. Sobarzo, *Crónica de la aventura,* 52-53. See also, *Daily Alta California,* August 15 and July 14, 1852, and *El Sonorense,* May 14, 1852.
49. *Daily Alta California,* August 15, October 18, 1852.
50. Lambertie, *Le drame de la Sonora,* 256-257.
51. Sobarzo, *Crónica de la aventura,* 61-64; Lambertie, *La drame de la Sonora,* 130-133; see also, Helen Broughall Metcalf, "The California French Filibusters in Sonora," *California Historical Quarterly,* 18 (March 1939), 3-21.
52. *El Sonorense,* September 24, 1852, Pinart Collection, Sonora, V, 64. See also, *Daily Alta California,* November 25, 1852, and Wyllys, *The French in*

Sonora, 73-74.

53. *Daily Alta California*, November 25, 1852.

54. *Ibid.*, December 23, 1852.

55. Sobarzo, *Crónica de la aventura*, 88-89.

56. Prefectura del partido de salvación to Governor of Sonora, Guaymas, August 15, 1852, L-E-17-11-65, 47-48, ASRE; see also, *Daily Alta California*, May 24, 1852.

57. Lambertie, *Le drame de la Sonora*, 22-23.

58. Fernando Cubillas, governor of Sonora, Ures, to prefect of Salvación, June 21, 1852; *El Sonorense*, June 25, 1852, Pinart Collection, Sonora, V, 32.

59. *New York Daily Times*, October 25 and December 17, 1852.

60. Lambertie, *Le drame de la Sonora*, 36-37; *Daily Alta California*, November 10, 1852.

61. Blanco to Cubillas, Arizpe, October 2, 1852; *El Sonorense*, October 8, 1852, Pinart Collection, Sonora, V, 67-81.

62. Lambertie, *Le drame de la Sonora*, 75-76; Wyllys, *The French in Sonora*, 111-112.

63. *Daily Alta California*, December 23, 1852; Wyllys, *The French in Sonora*, 121-122.

64. *El Sonorense*, November 12, 1852, Pinart Collection, Sonora, V, 110.

65. Conkling, México, D.F., to Marcy, May 19, 1853, vol. 16, roll 17, RG 59.

66. Alamán, México, D.F., to Conkling, 17 May, 1853, *Ibid.*

67. A. De Lachapelle, *Le comte de Raousset-Boulbon et l'expedition de la Sonora* (Paris: E. Dentu, 1859), 138.

68. Raousset Boulbon to Patrice Dillon, San Francisco, September 23, 1854, in *Daily Alta California*, September 24, 1854; Lachapelle, *Le comte*, 143-144.

69. Lachapelle, *Le comte*, 153-154.

70. Governor of Sonora, Ures, to SRE, Ures, May 8, 1854, L-E-6-2-19, 142-143, AHSRE. See also, *El Nacional* (Ures), March 17, 1854, 225, Pinart Collection, Sonora, V, 140, 225.

71. Sobarzo, *La crónica de la aventura*, 173; Lachapelle, *Le comte*, 163-164.

72. John E. Wool, San Francisco, to Jefferson Davis, Sec. of War, March 1, 1854, *Senate Exec. Doc. 16*, 33 Cong., 2nd sess., Serial 751, 11-12.

73. Sobarzo, *La crónica de la aventura*, 181.

74. *Daily Alta California*, September 30, November 2, 1854.

75. Sobarzo, *La crónica de la aventura*, 186-188; Lachapelle, *Le comte*, 177;

Daily Alta California, September 30, 1854.

76. *El Nacional*, July 15, 1854, 236-240.

77. José M. Yáñez, "Detalles y Algunos Documentos," *El Nacional* (México, D.F.), August 25, 1854, 243-246; Lachapelle, *Le comte*, 193-196.

78. José M. Yáñez, Guaymas, to Prefect, August 9, 1854, in *El Nacional*, September 1, 1854, Pinart Collection, V, 249.

79. Allen Johnson and Dumas Malone, eds., *Dictionary of American Biography*, 22 vols. (New York; Charles Scribner's Sons, 1928-1958), 363-365; Scroggs, *Filibusters and Financiers*.

80. William Walker, *The War in Nicaragua* (Mobile: S.H. Goetzel and Co., 1860), 19-20; see also, A. P. Nasatir, "The Second Incumbency of Jacques A. Morenhout," *California Historical Quarterly*, 27 (June 1948), 141-148.

81. Manuel Díaz de Bonilla, México, D.F., to James Gadsden, August 20, 1853, vol. 18, roll 19, RG 59.

82. W. A. Croffut, ed., *Fifty Years in Camp and Field: Diary of Ethan Allen Hitchcock, U.S.A.* (New York: G.P. Putnam's Sons, 1909), 400-403; see also, *Daily Alta California*, October 2, 1853.

83. *Daily Alta California*, October 11, 1853.

84. *Ibid.*, December 8, 1853.

85. *San Diego Herald*, December 3, 1853.

86. Juan Robinson, Guaymas, to James Gadsden, November 6, 1853, vol. 18, roll 19, RG-59.

87. James Gadsden, México, D.F., to Manuel Díaz de Bonillas, November 19,1853, *Ibid.*

88. *Daily Alta California*, December 16, 1853.

89. Arthur Woodward, ed., *The Republic of Lower California, 1853-1854, In the Words of its State Papers, Eyewitnesses, and Contemporary Reporters* (Los Angeles: Dawson's Book Store, 1966), 25-28.

90. Rufus K. Wyllys, "The Republic of Lower California, 1853-1854," *Pacific Historical Review*, 2 (June 1933), 194-213; Wyllys, "William Walker's Invasion of Sonora, 1854," *Arizona Historical Review*, 6 (October 1935), 61-67.

91. *Daily Alta California*, December 9, 1853.

92. *San Diego Herald*, December 3, 1853; *Daily Alta California*, December 8, 1853.

93. *Daily Alta California*, February 4, 22, 1854.

94. John E. Wool, Washington, to Jefferson Davis, January 10, 1854, *Senate*

Exec. Doc. 16, 33rd Cong., 2nd sess., Serial 751, 7.
95. *Los Angeles Star*, April 22, 1854.
96. *San Diego Herald*, May 5, 1854.

4: 1855-1860

1. Most of the correspondence for the Zerman filibustering attempt can be found in Ramo Justicia, Legajo 225, Tomo 674, Legajo 226, Tomo 675, and Tomo 677, Archivo General de la Nación, Lecumberri. Hereafter referred to as AGN.
2. Biographical information about Zerman is in Jorge Flores D., "La expedición filibustera de Juan Napoleón Zerman," *Documentos para la historia de la Baja California, papeles históricas mexicanas,* Tomo 2 (México, D.F., 1940), 33-65. See also, Eugene K. Chamberlain, "Baja California After Walker: The Zerman Enterprise," *Hispanic American Historical Review*, 34 (May 1954), 175-189.
3. Many of the facts for this chapter are from a report written by P. Sánchez Castro, sub-secretary of justicia. The report is forty-nine pages long, not dated, nor addressed. It might have been an internal memorandum or intended for the United States authorities in Mexico. See Legajo 225, Tomo 674, Justicia, AGN, 1-2. Hereafter cited as Sánchez Castro Doc. Some documentation is in AHSRE Fil-10-(I), 1858-1861. The extensive file on Zerman has to do with confiscation of his property and his attempts to retrieve whatever he could through the Mexican court system.
4. *Ibid.*, 6-20.
5. P.H. Cooley, Washington, to Ministro de Justicia, May 22, 1856, Legajo 225, Tomo 674, n.p.
6. Sánchez Castro Doc. *Ibid.*, 22-24.
7. John Forsyth, México, D.F., to Miguel Lerdo de Tejada, November 19, 1856, 80-83, Tomo 674, Legajo 225, AGN.
8. For U.S. concern about Andrews, see also John Forsyth, México, D.F., to Luis de La Rosa, Sec. of Relaciones Exteriores, March 6, 1856, *Ibid.*, n.p.
9. Forsyth, México, D.F., to Marcy, October 31, 1856, vol. 19, roll 20, vol. 20, roll 21, RG 59.
10. *Ibid.*
11. Forsyth, México, D.F., to Antonio de la Fuente, November 19, 1856, *Ibid.*

12. Forsyth, México, D.F., to Lerdo de Tejada, December 1, 1856, *Ibid.*

13. Lerdo de Tejada, México, D.F., to Forsyth, January 21, 1857, *Ibid.*

14. *Daily Alta California,* January 27, June 11, July 30, 1856.

15. Rufus K. Wyllys, "Henry A. Crabb: A Tragedy of the Sonora Frontier," *Pacific Historical Review,* 9 (June 1940), 184.

16. José de Aguilar, *Vindicación de su conducta,* Pinart Collection, V, 265.

17. For more on Pesqueira see, Rodolfo F. Acuña, *Sonoran Strongman: Ignacio Pesqueira and his Times* (Tucson: University of Arizona Press, 1974); Wyllys, "Henry A. Crabb," 86.

18. Robert H. Forbes, *Crabb's Expedition Into Sonora* (Tucson: Arizona Silhouttes, 1952), 8.

19. Manuel Robles Pezuela, Washington, to SRE, February 20, 1857, 1-4, Fil-9-(I), AHSRE; see also, John Forsyth, México, D.F., to Lewis Cass, April 24, 1857, vol. 20, roll 21, RG-59.

20. Henry A. Crabb, Sonoita, to Don José María Redondo, March 26, 1857, *House Exec.Doc.,* 64, 31.

21. *Datos históricos sobre filibusteros de 1857, en Caborca, Son* (Caborca, Sonora: Comité Organizador de las Fiestas del 6 de abril, 1926), 10; see also, *Estandarte Nacional* (México, D.F.), April 24, 1857.

22. *New York Daily Times,* May 19, 21, 1857; see also, *Datos Históricos,* 11.

23. Sworn Statement of Charles Edward Evans in correspondence, Charles B. Smith, Mazatlán, to John Forsyth, September 14, 1857, in *House Exec. Doc.,* 64, 65.

24. Forbes, *Crabb's Expedition,* 21; see also, *Daily Alta California,* August 3, 1857.

25. Statement of Evans in Smith to Forsyth, *House Exec. Doc.,* 64, 66, 73-74.

26. *Daily Alta California,* May 28, June 13, 1857.

27. John Forsyth, México, D.F., to D. Juan Antonio de la Fuente, SRE, May 30, 1857, 37-39, Fil-9-(I), AHSRE.

28. Gral. José M. Yáñez, Sr., comandante gral del estado de Sonora, Guaymas, nd. to gral. Luis Noreiga, Sr., comandante del division noroeste, *Ibid.,* 60-61. Here Yáñez explains the activities of the Crabb party and the breaking of Mexican law. He offers no excuses.

29. Alamán, México, D.F., to Conkling, May 17, 1853, vol.16, roll 17, RG-59.

30. Conkling, México, D.F., to Alamán, May 18, 1853, *Ibid.*

31. Conkling, México, D.F., to William Marcy, May 19, 1853, *Ibid.*

32. *Ibid.*, May 5, 1853, vol.17, roll 18.

33. *El Universal*, October 30, 1853, vol.18, roll 19, *Ibid.*

34. Gadsden, México, D.F., to Bonilla, August 22, 1853, vol. 18, roll 19, *Ibid.*

35. Gadsden, México, D.F., to Marcy, December 16, D.F., 1853, *Ibid.*

36. *Ibid.*, October 2, 1854.

37. *Ibid.*, November 5, 1855.

38. Forsyth, México, D.F., to Lewis Cass, April 24, 1857, vol. 20, roll 21.

39. *Ibid.*, May 7, 1857.

40. *Ibid.*, Sept. 15, 1857, vol. 21, roll 22.

41. *Ibid.*, March 18, 1858.

42. Luis G.Cuevas, México, D.F., to Forsyth, April 12, 1858, *Ibid.*

43. C.A. Bridges, "The Knights of the Golden Circle: A Filibustering Fantasy," *Southwestern Historical Quarterly*, 44 (January 1941), 285-302.

44. Roy Sylvan Dunn, "The KGC in Texas, 1860-1861," *Southwestern Historical Quarterly*, 70 (April 1967), 543-573. For an explanation of what the U.S. Army was doing along the border at the time and for additional information about this group and other border problems, see, Jerry Thompson, ed., *Fifty Miles and a Fight: Major Samuel Peter Heintzelman's Journal of Texas and the Cortina War* (Austin: Texas State Historical Association, 1998). See also, Jerry Thompson, ed., *Juan Cortina and the Texas-Mexico Frontier, 1859-1877* (El Paso: Texas Western Press, Southwestern Studies 99, 1994).

45. Dunn, "The KGC in Texas," 550.

5: 1855-1860

1. Many sources exist. For international relations see, Arnold Blumberg, *The Diplomacy of the Mexican Empire, 1863-1867* (Philadelphia: The American Philosophical Society, 1971).

2. Díaz's control of the country was aided by his "Rurales" police force. Paul J. Vanderwood, *Disorder and Progress: Bandits, Police, and Mexican Development* (Lincoln: University of Nebraska Press, 1981); see also, Agustín Aragón, *Porfirio Díaz*, 2 vols. (México, D.F.: Editora Intercontinental, 1950).

3. Thomas F. Corwin, México, D.F., to W. H. Seward, June 29, 1861, vol. 28, roll 29, RG-59.

4. For information on colonization see, Susana Glanz, *El ejido colectivo de*

nueva Italia (México, D.F.: Centro de Investigaciones Superiores, Instituto Nacional de Antropología e Historia, 1974). See also, Moisés González Navarro, *La colonización en México, 1877-1910* (México, D.F.: Talleres de Impresión de Estampillas y Valores, 1960).

5. For an overview of the period see, Clarence C. Clendenen, *Blood on the Border: The United States Army and the Mexican Irregulars* (New York: The Macmillan Co., 1969); and Martínez, *Troublesome Border.*

6. Frederick Merk, *Manifest Destiny And Mission in American History: A Reinterpretation* (New York: Alfred Knopf, 1963), 247, 263.

7. John B. Weller, México, D.F., to Don Francisco Zareb [illegible], March 16, 1861, L-E-1097, H/200 72:73 1., 8-9, AHSRE.

8. Matías Romero, Washington, to SRE, April 1861, *Ibid.*, 15-16.

9. *Ibid.*, March 5, 1861, 39-40.

10. *Ibid.*, 41-42.

11. *Ibid.*, June 4, 1861, 23.

12. *Ibid.*, August 16, 1861.

13. For additional information about Gwin see, Lately Thomas, *Between Two Empires: The Life Story of California's First Senator, William McKendree Gwin* (Boston: Houghton-Mifflin, 1969). For the best researched work on Gwin, see, Ana Rosa Suárez Argüello, *Un duque norteamericano para Sonora* (México, D.F.: Dirección General de Publicaciones del Consejo Nacional para la Cultura y las Artes, 1990).

14. Evan J. Coleman, ed., "Senator Gwin's Plan for the Colonization of Sonora," *Overland Monthly*, 17 (1891) 606. All the correspondence relating to Gwin's plan for Sonora was published in *Overland Monthly* between January and December, 1891. See also, Ana Rosa Suárez Argüello, "William M. Gwin: Su proyecto de colonización del noreste de México (1864-1865)," *Secuencia: Revista Americana de Ciencias Sociales* (Enero/Abril 1986), 134-142.

15. Gwin to Maximilian, Paris, September, 1863, *Overland Monthly*, second series, 17, 363, 497. See also, Hallie M. McPherson, "The Plan of William McKendree Gwin for a Colony in North Mexico, 1863-1865," *Pacific Historical Review*, 2 (December 1933), 461.

16. Lately Thomas, "The Operator and the Emperors," *American Heritage,* 15 (April 1964), 4-23, 82-83. See also, Gwin, Paris, to Napoleón III, January 5, 1864, *Overland Monthly*, 17, 501.

17. *New York Daily Times*, May 2, 1865; McPherson, "The Plan of William

Gwin," 369.

18. William M. Gwin, México, D.F. to his son, July 27, 1864, *Overland Monthly*, 18, second series, 204.

19. William M. Gwin, México, D.F., to Napoleón III, September 12, 1864, *Overland Monthly*, 17, 18, 506-507; William M. Gwin to his daughter, México, September 29, 1864, *Ibid.*, 509.

20. William M. Gwin, Paris, to Napoleón III, March 25, 1865, *Ibid.*, 515.

21. *Ibid.*, México, July 3, 1865, 596.

22. Thomas F. Corwin, México, D.F., to W. H. Seward, August 29, 1864, vol. 30, roll 31, RG-59.

23. E. D. Townsend, Washington, to P. Sheridan, April 13, 1866, *The War of the Rebellion: A Compilation of the Official Records of the Union and Confederate Armies*, 8, 897.

24. W. H. Seward, Washington, to J. Bigelow, July 13, 1865, *House Exec. Doc. 73*, 39 Cong., 1 sess., 539.

25. *San Francisco Chronicle*, May 24, 1890.

26. Matías Romero, Washington, to SRE, July 20, 1867, Fil-1-(I), 34, AHSRE.

27. Harry Bernstein, *Matías Romero, 1837-1898* (México, D.F.: Fondo de Cultura Económico, second edition, 1982).

28. Several sources exist that include colonization. See, for example, Moisés González Navarro, *Los extranjeros en México y los mexicanos en el extranjero, 1821-1920*, 3 tomos (México, D.F.: El Colegio de México, 1994). There were colonization efforts that Mexico approved in the 1860s. In 1864, the Juárez government granted Jacob P. Leese such a permit. This and other projects failed when few *norteños* migrated to Baja California. By 1871, only twenty-one American families lived in the region.

29. *La asociación del pueblo* (Guaymas), February 24, 1871, in Fil-1-(I), 48-49; *The New Mexican* (Santa Fe), January 20, 1871, *Ibid.*

30. A. Willard, Guaymas, to Thomas H. Nelson, November 18, 1870, vol. 42, roll 43, RG-59.

31. Ignacio Mariscal, Ministro de Gobernación, México, D.F., to SRE, May 28, 1872, *Ibid.*, 54.

32. L. M. Avendarro [?], México, D.F., to SRE, April 1873, *Ibid.*, 117-121.

33. Ignacio Mejía, México, D.F., to SRE, January 10, 1873, *Ibid.*, 70-73.

34. José María LaFragua, México, D.F., to SRE, April 18, 1874, *Ibid.*, 93-94.

35. John W. Foster, México, D.F., to Hamilton Fish, December 14, 1874,

vol. 53, roll 51, RG-59.

36. *Ibid.,* May 9, 1874.

37. Mexican Consul, Galveston, Texas, to SRE, June 13, 1874, *Ibid.,* 105.

38. Ignacio Mejía, México, D.F., to SRE, July 29, 1875, *Ibid.,* 112.

39. José María LaFragua, México, D.F. to SRE, July 31, 1875, *Ibid.,* 117.

40. John W. Foster, México, D.F., to Hamilton Fish, March 19, 1877, vols. 57-58, roll 55, RG-59.

41. Ignacio Mariscal, New York, to SRE, August 20, 1875, *Ibid.,* 120.

42. T. L. Vallarta, México, D.F. to Ignacio Mariscal, March 31, 1877, Fil-1-(II), 2, AHSRE.

43. Andrés Tapia [illegible], Consul at La Paz, to SRE, n.d., 1877, Fil-1-(III), *Ibid.,* 45.

44. John W. Foster, México, D.F., to William Evarts, November 12, 1877, vol. 60, roll 57, RG-59, RDS.

45. Michael G. Webster, "Intrigue on the Rio Grande: The Rio Bravo Affair, 1875," *Southwestern Historical Quarterly,* 74 (October 1970), 149-164.

46. Manuel María Zamacona, México, D.F., to SRE, April 17, 1880, Fil-12-(1), 1, AHSRE.

47. *National Free Press* (Washington), February 7, 1880, *Ibid.,* 4.

48. *Chronicle* (San Francisco), May 17, 1880, *Ibid.,* 9.

49. Rafael Varrios [Farrias?], Tucson, to SRE, August 6, 1880; Joaquín G. Conde, Washington, to SRE, June 21, 1880; Juan N. Navarro, Mexican Consul in New York City, to SRE, June 26, 1880, Fil-12-(1), 1, 30, *Ibid.,* 15-16.

50. *News Letter* (San Francisco), May 23, 1880, *Ibid.,* 10.

51. *Evening Bulletin* (San Francisco), August 7, 1880, *Ibid.,* n.p.

52. *Daily Alta California,* August 6, 1880.

53. *Ibid.,* August 7, 1880.

54. Dr. Plutarco Ornelas, Mexican Consul, San Antonio, to SRE, August 10, 1880, 35-47; Ornelas, San Antonio, to Joaquín G. Conde, August 6, 1880, 60-61, in Fil 12-(1), 1, AHSRE.

55. La Collección General Porfirio Díaz, Legajo V, Documents 3166-68, 3188, Universidad de las Américas, Puebla.

56. Plutarco Ornelas, San Antonio, to Governor of Texas, August 20, 1880, Fil 12-(1), 67-70, AHSRE.

57. Plutarco Ornelas, San Antonio, to SRE, September 26, 1880, *Ibid.,* 89-95.

58. Matías Romero, Washington, to SRE, May 4, 1886, Fil-1-(II), *Ibid.,* 78-79.

59. Cayetano Romero (brother of Matías), Washington, to SRE, March 9, 1886, *Ibid.,* 107-109.

60. *New York Times,* September 20, 1886; José V. Dozal, El Paso, Texas, to SRE, Fil-13-(I), *Ibid.,* 103.

61. *Daily New Mexican,* August 17, 18, 24, 1886.

62. *Ibid.,* August 17, 1886.

63. Henry R. Jackson, México, D.F., to Ignacio Mariscal, July 6, 1886, no. 266, vol. 90, roll 85, RG. 59; Jackson, México, D.F., to Thomas F. Bayard, Sec. of State, *Ibid.,* no. 278.

64. J. Escobar, El Paso, to SRE, October 26, 1886, *Ibid.,* 11; *The Daily Times* (El Paso), October 27, 1886.

65. Matías Romero, New York, to SRE, October 28, 1886, *Ibid.,* no. 266.

66. *New York Herald,* November 11, 1886, *Ibid.,* 19.

67. *Chicago Times,* November 12, 1886, *Ibid.,* 30.

68. *Ibid.*

69. Manuel G. Zamora, New Orleans, to SRE, November 16, 1886, *Ibid.,* 40-41.

70. M. Rahden, Mexican Consul in Kansas City, to SRE, November 22, 1886, *Ibid.,* 54-55.

71. Matías Romero, Washington, to SRE, November 24, 1886, *Ibid.,* 60-61.

72. Jackson, México, D.F., to Bayard, August 27, 1886, no. 304, *Ibid.*

73. A.K. Coney, San Franciso, to SRE, April 16, 17, 1889, Fil-1-(III), 8, AHSRE.

74. Whether this group was the same as the Knights of the Golden Circle is not clear. There are no comments in the archives of the Secretaría de Relaciones Exteriores in México, D.F., that mentioned this, but it was probably the same party. The KGC organized in California shortly before the Civil War.

75. *Los Angeles Chronicle,* April 14, 1889, 1-7, Fil-1-(III), 1-7, AHSRE.

76. A. K. Coney, San Francisco, to SRE, April 16, 17, 1889, *Ibid.,* 8.

77. Matías Romero, Washington, to SRE, April 18, 1889, Fil-1-(III), *Ibid.,* 21-24.

78. A. K. Coney, San Francisco, to SRE, April 22, 1889, *Ibid.,* 27.

79. Matías Romero, New York, to A. K. Coney, May 2, 1889, *Ibid.,* 67-69.

80. Some of the newspaper articles concerning the filibustering of 1888-1890 can be found in Anna Marie Hager, ed., *The Filibusters of 1890: The Captain John F. Janes and Lower California Newspaper Reports and the Walter*

G. Smith Manuscript (Los Angeles: Dawson's Book Store, 1968). This work contains much of the same information that Secretaría de Relaciones Exteriores Archivo has gathered. The documents in the Mexican archive, however, are more complete.
81. A. K. Coney, San Francisco, to SRE, May 23, 1890, Fil-1-(III), AHSRE, *Ibid.*, 151-152.

6: 1890-1921

1. See, David Healy, *U.S. Expansionism: The Imperialist Urge in the 1890s* (Madison: University of Wisconsin Press, 1970), and Julius W. Pratt, *The Expansionists of 1898: The Acquisition of Hawaii and the Spanish Islands* (New York: The Macmillan Co., 1951).
2. A. C. Vázquez, Havana, Cuba, to SRE, May 23, 1890, Fil-1-(III), 138-139, ASRE. See also, Andrew F. Rolle, "Futile Filibustering in Baja California, 1888-1890," *Pacific Historical Review*, 20 (May 1951), 159-166.
3. Los Angeles, *Tribune*, April 19, 1889.
4. *San Diego Union*, May 21, 1890. See also, *Washington Post*, May 22, 1890, and *New York Tribune*, May 22, 1890. Copies of these newspapers were in Fil-1-(III), AHSRE.
5. *La República Mexicana* (México, D.F.), May 24, 1890, *Ibid.*
6. *San Diego Union*, May 21, 1890, *Ibid.*
7. Tomás Valdespina Figueroa, San Diego, to SRE, May 22, 1890, Fil-1-(III), *Ibid.*, 146-148.
8. *San Diego Union*, May 22, 1890.
9. Luis E. Torres, Ensenada, to Porfirio Díaz, May 23, 1890, Fil-1-(III), *Ibid.*, 143-148.
10. Matías Romero, Washington, to SRE, May 22, 1890, *Ibid.*, 130-132.
11. *Ibid.*, June 10, 1890, 206-207.
12. *Ibid.*, May 23, 1890, 146-147.
13. Tomás Valdespina Figueroa, San Diego, to SRE, May 26, 1890, *Ibid.*, 159. The telegram was sent to SRE and then to Romero.
14. *San Diego Union*, May 25, 1890, *Ibid.*, 164.
15. *San Francisco Chronicle*, May 25, 1890. See also, A. K. Coney, San Francisco, to SRE, May 26, 1890, *Ibid.*, 166-167.
16. *Ibid.*

17. *San Diego Republic*, May 24, 1890; Tomás Valdespina Figueroa, San Diego, to SRE, May 28, 1890, both in *Ibid.*, 171-172.

18. Manuel de Aspíroz, Ensenada, to Jefe Político del Norte de la Baja California, June 9, 1890, Fil-1-(IV), 200-201, AHSRE.

19. Matías Romero, Washington, to SRE, June 10, 1890, *Ibid.*, 230-231.

20. *Ibid.*, May 31, 1890, Fil-1-(III), 177-179.

21. A. K. Coney, San Francisco, to SRE, June 10, 1890, *Ibid.*, 42-43; *San Francisco Chronicle*, June 10, 1890, *Ibid.*

22. *San Francisco Chronicle*, June 11, 1890, *Ibid.,* 45-49.

23. Matías Romero, Washington, to SRE, June 12, 1890, *Ibid.*, 55-59.

24. A. K. Coney, San Francisco, to SRE, June 18, 1890, *Ibid.*, 82-83.

25. Matías Romero, Washington, to SRE, June 20, 1890, *Ibid.*, 98-99.

26. *San Francisco Chronicle*, June 3, 4, 1890.

27. Matías Romero, Washington, to SRE, June 21, 1890, *Ibid.*, 106-108.

28. A. K. Coney, San Francisco, to SRE, June 5, 1890, *Ibid.*, 179-180.

29. Matías Romero, Washington, to SRE, July 1, 1890, *Ibid.*, 147-150.

30. *Ibid.*, June 10, 1890, 230-231.

31. A. K. Coney San Francisco, to SRE, June 11, 1890, *Ibid.*, 245-247; see also, *San Francisco Chronicle*, June 12, 1890, *Ibid.*

32. *San Francisco Chronicle*, June 18, 1890, *Ibid.,* 82-83

33. John W. Foster, Washington, to Matías Romero, June 21, 1890, *Ibid.*, 109-112.

34. Cayetano Romero, Washington, to SRE, July 9, 1891, Fil-14-(I), 7-9, AHSRE.

35. A. K. Coney, San Francisco, to SRE, September 10, 1895, Fil-15-(I), *Ibid.*, l.

36. Matías Romero, New York, to SRE, September 16, 1895, *Ibid.* 5-6.

37. *Ibid.*, September 24, 1895, 25-27. See also, *The Mail and Express* (New York), September 25, 1895, included in the Romero communication.

38. *Ibid.*, September 26, 1895, 38-39; A. K. Coney, San Francisco, to SRE, September 30, 1895; *Ibid.*, 42, 43; Matías Romero, Washington, to SRE, October 17, 1895, *Ibid.*

39. Eduardo Ruíz, Consul at San Diego, to SRE, August 11, 1921, Fil-16-(I), 7, *Ibid.*

40. Agustín Piña, Phoenix, Arizona, to SRE, May 7, 1903, in "Conspiración filibustera contra autoridades de la Cananea, Sonora," L-E-15-10-20, *Ibid.*

41. Manuel de Aspíroz, Washington, to John Hay, June 5, 1903, *Ibid.*

42. Frederick S. Nair, United States Attorney, Washington, to Attorney General, July 3, 1903, *Ibid.*

43. Díaz Prieto, consul San Diego, to SRE, October 28, 1907, in "Tiburon," supuesta expedición, L-E-15-19-4, 1-2, *Ibid.*

44. *Ibid.*, November 27, 1907.

45. Lowell L. Blaisdell, "Was it Revolution or Filibustering? The Mystery of the Flores Magón Revolt in Baja California," *Pacific Historical Review,* 23 (May 1954), 147-164.

46. Lowell Blaisdell, *The Desert Revolution: Baja California, 1911* (Madison: University of Wisconsin Press, 1961), treats the attempts to organize filibustering expeditions as not serious. He is correct from the U.S. point of view. For the Mexican perspective see, Rómulo Velasco Ceballos, *¿Se apoderá Estados Unidos de América de Baja California?; La invasion filibustera, 1911* (México, D.F.: Imprenta Nacional, 1920). Also see, Peter Gerhard, "The Socialist Invasion of Baja California, 1911," *Pacific Historical Review,* 15 (September 1946), 295-304.

47. See, Lawrence Douglas Taylor, *La gran aventura en México,* 2 tomos (México, D.F.: Consejo Nacional Para la Cultura y las Artes, 1993), tomo 1, 203-210.

48. Tasker H. Bliss, Camp Lakeside, California, to War Department, May 18, 1911, 812.00/1933, United States Department of State, *Records Relating to Internal Affairs of Mexico, 1910-1920,* RG 59, Series 812.00 Microfilm Publications, Microcopy 274, National Archives, Washington, D.C. Hereafter cited as Mexico: Internal Affairs, 812.00, RG 59.

49. Secretary of State, Washington, to Attorney General, May 20, 1911, 812.00/1934, *Ibid.*

50. M. de Zamacona, Washington, to Secretary of State, May 11, 1911, 812.00/1880, *Ibid.*

51. Plutarco Ornelas, Mexican Consul in San Francisco, to SRE, February 7, 1911, "Expedición filibustera en la Baja California," 16-6-7, primera parte, 10, AHSRE.

52. A. I. McCormick, U. S. Attorney, Los Angeles, California, to Attorney General, May 31, 1911, Mexico: Internal Affairs, 812.00/2089, RG-59.

53. M. de Zamacona, Mexican Ambassador, Washington, to Secretary of State, May 24, 1911, 812.00/1952, *Ibid.*

54. Díaz Prieto, no location, to SRE, June 5, 1911, 16-6-7, primera parte,

215-224, AHSRE.

55. Asst. Attorney General, Washington, to Sec. of State, April 19, 1911, Mexico: Internal Affars, 812.00/1371, RG-59. Special Agent Herrington, Bureau of Investigation, Department of Justice reports to the justice department that Ferris is a clown and does not intend to enter Mexico for any reason.

56. Asst. Attorney General, Washington, to Sec. of State, March 23, 1911, Mexico: Internal Affairs, 812.00/1047, RG-59.

57. Lowell Blaisdell, "Harry Chandler and Mexican Border Intrigue, 1914-1917," *Pacific Historical Review*, 35 (Fall 1966), 385-393; Eugene K. Chamberlain, "Mexican Colonization Versus American Interests in Lower California," *Pacific Historical Review*, 20 (January 1951), 43-55.

58. "Revolución Mexicana Durante Los Anos de 1910 A 1920. Información diversas de la república y de los oficinas de México en el exterior," L-E 859, 5-143, AHSRE.

59. Eduardo Ruíz, San Diego, to SRE, August 11, 1921, in Fil-16-(I), *Ibid.*, 7.

60. *Ibid.*, September 1, 1921, 21-29.

61. For a complete discussion of this period see, Clifford N. Trow, "Senator Albert B. Fall and Mexican Affairs: 1912-1921," unpublished Ph.D. dissertation, University of Colorado, 1966.

62. General Albelardo L. Rodríquez, Mexicali, to Eduardo Ruíz, September 19, 1921, Fil-16-(I), 34-36, AHSRE.

63. SRE, México, D.F., to Alvaro Obregón, October 21, 1921, *Ibid.*, 42.

64. *San Diego Sun*, November 8, 1921, *Ibid.*

65. E. Ferriera, San Diego, to SRE, November 12, 1921, Fil-16-(I), *Ibid.*, 127-128.

66. J. A. Ulloa, Consul at San Francisco, to E. Ferreira, December 27, 1921, *Ibid.*, 318-357.

67. E. Ferreira, San Diego, to SRE, November 19, 1921, *Ibid.*, 219-221.

68. *Ibid.*, November 20, 1921, 204, November 25, 1921, 268-269.

69. *Ibid.*, December 7, 1921, 291-292. W. Dirk Raat in *Revoltosos* suggests that the United States selectively enforced its neutrality laws during the Mexican Revolution. He is correct for events from 1848 to 1921.

70. A particularly insightful work, John Mason Hart, *Revolutionary Mexico: The Coming and Process of the Mexican Revolution* (Los Angeles: University of California Press, 1987), provides an understanding of the influence of foreign economic penetration into Mexico as a promoter of revolution.

BIBLIOGRAPHY

Government Documents: Mexico
Primary Sources: Documents from the Archivo Genaro Estrada de la Secretaría de Relaciones Exteriores (México, D.F).: "Relación de Expedientes sóbre Filibusterismo":

L-E-859
L-E-l096
L-E-l097
15-19-4
16-6-7

FIL-I-(I)

1867—La Legación Méxicana en Washington informa sobre las expediciones filibusteras que se organizan en Nueva York y Nueva Orleans contra México. Medidas tomadas por el gobierno de los E.U.A. para impedir dichas expediciones. ff. 33-46.
1871—el Gobierno del Estado de Jalisco envía un ejemplar del periódico "La Asociación del Pueblo" que publica los rumores de una expedición filibustera organizada en Arizona para invadir el territorio Mexicano con el proyecto de fundar la "República del Pacífico." ff. 47-50.
1872-74—Documentos relativos a la ocupación de una parte del territorio

de la Baja California (Salinas de Ojo de Libre y San Quintín) por una partida de filibusteros. ff. 51-69.

1873—Informes de Consulados en los E. U.A. sobre los preparativos de expediciones filibusteras para invadir los Estados de Sonora y Chihuahua. ff. 70-91.

1874—El Consul Mexicano en Galveston remite tiras de periódicos que tratan de la extradición de Alexander D. Hamilton y noticias sobre la propaganda filibustera que tiene por objeto el establecimiento de la República de la "Sierra Madre" integrada por los estados mexicanos fronterizos. ff. 92-109.

1875—El Gobierno de Coahuila informa que en la banda opuesta del Bravo se encuentra una reunión de filibusteros con el objeto de invadir el Estado de Coahuila. ff. 110-121.

FIL-1-(II)

1877—Datos e informes de las autoridades de Baja California sobre la organización de filibusteros en San Francisco para invadir el territorio Mexicano. ff. 1-52.

1877-1878—Testimonio de la averiguación levantada ante el Juzgado de Distrito del Norte de Tamaulipas, por orden del ministerio de Justicia, sobre filibusterismo e invasiones del territorio nacional. ff. 53-76.

1886—El Consulado de México en San Diego comunica noticias sobre el proyecto de una expedición filibustera con dirección a la Baja California para la formación del nuevo estado de "Marvista." ff. 79-119.

1887—Entrevista del Sr. Matías Romero, Ministro de México en Washington con el Secretario de Estado Mr.Bayard sobre algunas cuestiones pendientes de carácter internacional entre México y los E.U.A. (Bergantín "Rebecca" y Caso Cutting). ff. 120-131.

FIL-1-(III)

1889-1890—Manuel Sánchez Facio y Manuel Tinoco. Los cónsules en San Francisco y en San Diego California, comunican y envían recortes de periódicos sóbre la organización de una expedición de filibusteros en complicidad con Manuel Sánchez Facio y Manual Tinoco para ocupar la península de la Baja California y anexarla a los E.U.A. ff. 181.

FIL-1-(IV)

1890—Manuel Sánchez Facio y Manuel Tinoco. Los cónsules en San Francisco y San Diego, California, comunican y envían recortes de periódicos sobre la organización de una expedición de filibusteros en complicidad con Manuel Sánchez Facio y Manuel Tinoco para ocupar la península de la Baja California y anexarla a los E.U.A. ff. 1-186.

FIL-3-(I)

1840-47—Francisco Sentmanat. Intercambio de correspondencia entre México y Nueva Orleans sobre la expedición de Francisco Sentmanat y su fusilamiento en Tabasco. ff. 1-35. Reclamación de Inglaterra y España por la muerte y prisión de sus ciudadanos integrantes de la expedición de Francisco Sentmanat. ff. 36-125.

FIL-5-(V)

1854—Gastón de Raousset,Conde de Boulbon.Expedición projectada por el Conde Gastón Raousset de Boulbon en San Francisco, California, contra el Estado de Sonora y Baja California. ff. 224.

FIL-7-(II)

1851-1852—José María J.Carvajal.Comunicaciones dirigidas al Ministro de Relaciones con motivo de la invasión filibustera de José María J. Carvajal en la frontera de Tamaulipas con el fin de formarla las reclamaciones que sean conveniente al gobierno de los Estados Unidos de América. ff. 182.

FIL-7-(V)

1852—José María J.Carvajal. Expediciones filibusteras al mando de José María J.Carvajal, para ocupar la frontera de México y formar con los Estados del Norte "La República de la Sierra Madre." ff. 163.

FIL-7-(VI)

1853—José María J. Carvajal. Expediciones filibusteras al mando de José María J.Carvajal organizadas en territorio de los E.U.A. para ocupar la frontera de México y formar con los Estados del Norte "La República de la Sierra Madre." Aprehensión y juicio en contra de José María J.Carvajal y sus acómplices. ff. 132.

FIl-7-(VII)

1854—José María J.Carvajal. Juicio en contra de José María J. Carvajal por haber violado las Leyes de Neutralidad de los E.U.A. con las expediciones filibusteras en contra del territorio Mexicano. Informes sobre los movimientos revolucionarios en la frontera para organizar una nueva expedición en contra de México. ff. 155.

FIL-7-(VIII)

1855-1873—Informes sobre la organización de movimientos filibusteros en los E.U.A. al mando de José María J.Carvajal para ocupar los estados de la frontera de México y formar una nueva república. ff. 1-140.
Expedientes formados sobre las invasiones de americanos al territorio de México encabezados por José María J. Carvajal. ff. 141-279.

FIL-9-(I)

1857—Enrique A. Crabb. El Ministro de México en los Estados Unidos de América comunica noticias sobre la organización en la Alta California de una expedición al mando de Enrique A. Crabb para invadir el Estado de Sonora. Captura y fusilamiento de filibusteros. ff. 75.

FIL-12-(I)

1880—General Ernesto Dalrymple. Proyecto de invasión a México y Centro América procedente del Sur de Arizona y Texas por 50,000 filibusteros al mando del General Ernesto Dalrymple. ff. 102.

FIL-13-(I)

1886—A.K. Cutting. Proyecto filibustero encabezado por A. K. Cutting en conexión con Edward Friend para el establecimiento de una nación independiente que se denominara "República Socialista." ff. 98.

FIL-14-(I)

1891—Capitan Annett. La Legación de México en Washington comunica noticias sobre una expedición filibustera contra México organizada en Norfolk Estado de Virginia y encabezada por el Capitan Annett al mando de 200 hombres. ff. 12.

FIL-15-(1)

1895-96—Friers y Bethune. El cónsul de México en San Francisco informa que en Oakland se hacen los preparativos de la Goleta llamada "Satana" para una expedición filibustera a la Baja California por cuenta de Friers y Bethune. ff. 94.

FIL-16-(I)

1921—Actividades Filibusteras en contra de la Baja California. Consulados de México en los E.E. U.U. informan sóbre las actividades del ex-Capitan del ejército norteamericano Dineley, encargado de reclutar y amestrar a los filibusteros y de los movimientos encabezados por el Ex-Coronel Estéban Cantú para invadir las poblaciones fronterizas del Distrito Norte de la Baja California. ff. 179.

Informe de la comisión Pesquisidora de la frontera del norte al ejecutivo de la unión cumplimiento del artículo 3 de la ley de 30 de Septiembre de 1872 (Monterrey, México), Mayo 15 de 1872. Published México, D.F., Imprenta de Díaz de León y White, 1874 (original in AHSRE).

La Coleción General Porfirio Díaz, Legajo V, Docs. 3166-68, Universidad de las Américas, Cholula.

Ramo de Justicia, Legajo 225, tomo 674; Legajo 226, tomo 675, 677, Archivo General de la Nación, México, D. F.

Manuscripts, Unpublished:

Pinart, Alphonse. "Documents for the History of Sonora," Manuscripts and printed matter in the collection of Alphonse Pinart. Bancroft Library, University of California, Berkeley.

Government Documents: United States

House Executive Document, 50, 30 Cong., 2 sess., Serial 541.
House Executive Document, 64, 35 Cong., 1 sess., Serial 955.
House Executive Document, 73, 39 Cong., 1 sess., Serial 1261.
Senate Executive Document, 33 Cong, 2 sess., Serial 751.

Manning, William R. (ed.). *Diplomatic Correspondence of the United States, Inter-American Affairs, 1831-1860*, 12 vols., Washington, D.C., 1932-1939. United States Department of State. Dispatches from U.S. Ministers to Mexico, 1823-1906, Record Group 59, National Archives and Records Service. (Microfilm copy in Oklahoma State University Library, Stillwater.) United States Department of State. Consular Dispatches, Mazatlán, México, Record Group 59, National Archives. (Microfilm copy in Oklahoma State University Library, Stillwater.) United States Department of State. Consular Dispatches, Guaymas, Mexico, Record Group 59, National Archives. (Microfilm copy in Oklahoma State University Library, Stillwater.) *The War of the Rebellion: A Compilation of the Official Records of the Union and Confederate Armies.* 128 vols. Washington, D.C.: GPO, 1880-1901.

Newspapers

Brownsville, Texas, *Río Bravo*, AHSRE.
Brownsville, Texas, *La Bandera*, AHSRE.
Chicago, Illinois, *Times*, AHSRE.
El Paso, *The Daily Times*
Guaymas, Mexico, *La Asociación del Pueblo*, AHSRE.
Los Angeles, California, *Star*, AHSRE.
Los Angeles, California, *Chronicle*, AHSRE.

Los Angeles, California, *Tribune*, AHSRE.

México, D.F., *El Constitucional: Periódico Oficial*, AHSRE.

México D.F, *El Nacional*

México, D.F. *La República Mexicana*

México, D.F.,*Estandarte Nacional*, Ministerial Despatches, Record Group 59, United States Department of State, National Archives.

New Orleans, *Daily Picayune*

New York Daily Times

New York Herald

New York, *The Mail and Express*

New York Tribune

San Diego Herald, AHSRE.

San Diego Union, AHSRE.

San Diego Republic, AHSRE.

San Diego Sun, AHSRE.

San Francisco, *Daily Alta California*

San Francisco, *Chronicle*

San Francisco, *News Letter*

San Francisco, *Evening Bulletin*

Santa Fe, New Mexico, *The New Mexican*

Ures, Sonora, *El Sonorense*

Ures, Sonora, *El Nacional*

Washington, D.C., *National Free Press*

Washington Post

Miscellaneous Primary Documents:

Almonte, Juan N. *Proyecto de leyes sobre colonización*. México D.F., Imprenta de I. Cumplido, 1852.

Colonias militares, proyecto para su establecimiento en las fronteras de oriente y occidente de la república. México, D.F.: Imprenta de I. Cumplido, 1848.

Paredes, Mariano. *Proyectos de leyes sobre colonización y comercio en el estado de Sonora, presentados a la Cámara de Diputados por el representante de aquel estado, en la sesión extraordinario del día 16 de Agosto de 1850*. México, D.F. Imprenta de I. Cumplido, 1850.

Unpublished Works:

Campos Lamos, Alejando, "Catalogo de la serie filibusterismo del Archivo Histórico Genaro Estrada, 1835-1854," unpublished thesis, Universidad Nacional Autónoma de México, 1996.

Stevens, Robert C., "Forsaken Frontier: A History of Sonora, Mexico, 1821-1851," Ph.D. dissertation University of California, Berkeley, 1963.

Zamarano Navarro, Beatriz Eugenia, "Filibusteros norteamericanas en México, 1850-1860," M.A. Thesis, Universidad Autónoma Nacional de México, 1987.

Books:

Albro, Ward S. *Always a Rebel: Ricardo Flores Magón and the Mexican Revolution.* Fort Worth: Texas Christian University Press, 1992.

Acuña, Rodolfo F. *Sonoran Strongman: Ignacio Pesqueira and His Times.* Tucson: University of Arizona Press, 1974.

Aragón, Agustín. *Porfirio Díaz.* 2 tomos. México, D.F.: Editora Intercontinental, 1950.

Bancroft, Hubert Howe. *History of California.* 7 vols. San Francisco: The History Company, 1886-1890.

Bancroft, Hubert Howe. *History of the North Mexican States and Texas,* 2 vols. San Francisco: The History Company, 1884-1889.

Berstein, Harry. *Matías Romero, 1837-1898,* México, D.F.: Fondo de Cultura Económica, 1973, 1982.

Blaisdell, Lowell L. *The Desert Revolution: Baja California, 1911.* Madison: University of Wisconsin Press, 1961.

Blumberg, Arnold. *The Diplomacy of the Mexican Empire, 1863-1867.* Philadelphia: The American Philosophical Society, 1971.

Brown, Charles H. *Agents of Manifest Destiny: The Lives and Times of the Filibusters.* Chapel Hill: University of North Carolina Press, 1980.

Calcott, Wilfred H. *Liberalism in Mexico, 1857-1929.* Palo Alto: Stanford University Press, 1931.

Calazadíaz Barrera, Alberto. *Dos gigantes: Sonora y Chihuahua,* 2 tomos. Hermosillo, Sonora: Escritores Asociados del Norte, 1964.

Clendenen, Clarence C. *Blood on the Border: The United States Army and the*

Mexican Irregulars. New York: The Macmillan Company, 1969.

Cline, Howard F. *The United States and Mexico.* Cambridge: Harvard University Press, 1965.

Coerver, Don M. and Linda B. Hall. *Texas and the Mexican Revolution: A Study in State and National Border Policy, 1910-1920.* San Antonio: Trinity University Press, 1984.

Cosío Villegas, Daniel. *História moderna de México,* 7 tomos. México, D.F.: Editorial Hermes, 1953-1965.

John H. Coatsworth and Carlos Rico (eds.). *Images of Mexico in the United States.* San Diego: University of California at San Diego, 1989.

Croffut, W. A. (ed.). *Fifty Years in Camp and Field: The Diary of Ethan Allen Hitchcock, U.S.A.* New York: G.P. Putnam Son's, 1909.

Datos históricos sobre filibusteros de 1857, En Caborca, Son. Caborca, Sonora: Comité Organizador de las Fiestas del 6 de Abril, 1926.

DePalo, William A., Jr. *The Mexican National Army, 1822-1852.* College Station: Texas A&M University Press, 1997.

Forbes, Robert H. *Crabb's Expedition Into Sonora,1857.* Tucson: Arizona Silhouttes, 1952.

Francaviglia, Richard V. and Richmond, Douglas. *Dueling Eagles: Reinterpreting the U.S.-Mexican War, 1846-1848.* Fort Worth: Texas Christian University Press, 2000.

Fuentes Mares, José. *Y México se refugió en el desierto: Luis Terrazas: historia y destino México.* México, D.F.: Editorial Jus, 1954.

Fuller, John D. *The Movement for the Acquisition of all Mexico.* Baltimore: Johns Hopkins Press, 1936.

Garber, Paul N. *The Gadsden Treaty,* Philadelphia: University of Pennsylvania Press, 1923.

García Cantón, Gastón. *Invasiones norteamericanas en México.* México, D.F.: Serie Popular Era, 1971.

Glantz, Susana. *El ejido colectivo de nueva Italia.* México, D.F.: Centro de Investigaciones Superiores, Instituto Nacional de Antropología e Historia, 1974.

González Flores, Enrique. *Chihuahua de la independencia a la revolución.* México, D.F.:Ediciones Botas-México, 1949.

González Navarro, Moisés. *La colonización en México, 1877- 1910.* México, D.F.: Talleres de Impresión de Estampillas y Valores, 1960.

Greene, Lawrence. *The Filibuster: The Career of William Walker.*

Indianapolis: The Bobbs-Merrill Company, 1937.

Hager, Anna Marie. *The Filibusters of 1890, The Captain John F. Janes and Lower California Newspaper Reports and the Walter G. Smith Manuscript.* Los Angeles: Dawson's Book Store, 1968.

Hall, Linda B. and Don M. Coerver. *Revolution on the Border: The United States and Mexico, 1910-1920.* Albuquerque: University of New Mexico Press, 1988.

Hart, John Mason. *Revolutionary Mexico: The Coming and Process of the Mexican Revolution.* Los Angeles: University of California Press, 1987.

Healy, David. *U.S. Expansionism: The Imperialist Urge in the 1890s.* Madison: University of Wisconsin Press, 1970.

Johnson, Allen and Dumas Malone (eds.). *Dictionary of American Biography.* 22 vols. New York: Charles Scribner's Sons, 1928-1958.

Jordán, Fernando. *Crónica de un país bárbaro.* Chihuahua, Chihuahua: Centro Librero La Prensa, S.A. de C.V.. 1956.

Lachapelle, A. De. *Le comte de Raousset-Boulbon et L' expedition de la Sonora.* Paris: E. Dentu, 1859.

Lambert, Paul F. "The All Mexico Movement," in O. B. Faulk and Joseph A. Stout, Jr. (eds.). *The Mexican War: Changing Interpretations.* Chicago: Swallow Press, 1973.

Lambertie, Charles de. *Le drame de la Sonora, L' etat de Sonora, M. le comte de Raousset Boulbon et M. Charles de Pindray.* Paris: Chez Ledoyen, Libraie Editeur, 1885.

Martínez, Oscar J. *Border Boom Town: Ciudad Juárez Since 1848.* Austin: University of Texas Press,1975.

_____. *Troublesome Border.* Tucson: University of Arizona Press, 1988.

Martínez, Pablo L. *A History of Lower California.* First English translation. México: Editorial Baja California, 1960.

Merk, Frederick. *Manifest Destiny and Mission in American History.* New York: Alfred Knopf 1963.

Moore, John B. (ed.) *The Works of James Buchanan.* 12 vols. New York: Antiquarian Press, 1908-1911.

Moyano Pahissa, Angela. *México y Estados Unidos: Orígines de una relación, 1819-1861.* México, D.F: Secretaría de Educación Pública, 1985.

_____. *California y sus relaciones con Baja California.* México, D.F.: Fondo de Cultura Económica, 1983.

Oster, Patrick. *The Mexicans: A Personal Portrait of a People.* New York: William Morrow and Company, Inc., 1989.

Pratt, Julius. *The Expansionists of 1898: The Acquisition of Hawaii and the Spanish Islands.* New York: The Macmillan Company, 1951.

_____. *The Expansionists of 1812.* New York: The Macmillan Company, 1925.

Quaife, Milo M. (ed.) *James K. Polk, The Diary of James K. Polk During His Presidency, 1845-1849.* 4 vols. Chicago: A.C. Mclurg Company, 1910.

Raat, W. Dirk. *Revoltosos: Mexico's Rebels in the United States, 1903-1923.* College Station: Texas A&M University Press, 1981.

Reeves, Jesse S. *American Diplomacy Under Tyler and Polk.* Baltimore: The Johns Hopkins University Press, 1907.

Rippy, J. Fred. *The United States and Mexico.* New York: Alfred A. Knopf, 1926.

Robles, Vito Alessio. *Coahuila y Texas.* 2 tomos. México, D.F.: Editorial Porrúa, 1945.

Ruibal Corella, Juan Antonio. *Patriota: La buella del General Ignacio Pesqueira García en el noreste de México.* México, D.F.: Editorial Porrúa, 1979.

Santoni, Pedro. *Mexicans at Arms, Puro Federalists and the Politics of War, 1845-1848.* Ft. Worth: Texas Christian University Press, 1996.

Scholes, Walter V. *Mexican Politics During the Juárez Regime, 1855-1872.* Columbia: University of Missouri Press, 1957.

Schoonover, Thomas David. *Dollars Over Dominion: The Triumph of Liberalism in Mexican-United States Relations, 1861-1867.* Baton Rouge: Louisiana State University Press, 1978.

Scroggs, William O. *Filibusters and Financiers: The Story of William Walker and His Associates.* New York: The Macmillan Company, 1916.

Sierra, Justo. *Juárez, su obra y su tiempo.* México, D.F.: Editorial Porrúa, 1970.

Sobarzo, Horacio. *Crónica de la aventura de Raousset-Boulbon en Sonora.* México, D.F.: Librería de Manuel Porrúa, 1954.

Soulie, Maurice. *La gran aventura: L'epope de comte de Raousset- Boulbon au Mexique, 1850-1854.* Paris: Payot, 1926.

Stout, Joseph A. Jr. *The Liberators: Filibustering Expeditions into Mexico, 1848-1862, and the Last Thrust of Manifest Destiny.* Los Angeles: Westernlore Press, 1973.

Suárez Argüello, Ana Rosa. *Un duque norteamericano para Sonora.* México, D.F.: Consejo Nacional para la Cultura y las Artes, 1990.

Symons, Farrell (trans.). *The Wolf Cub: The Great Adventure of Count de Raousset-Boulbon in California and Sonora, 1850-1854*. By Maurice Soulie, Indianapolis: Bobbs-Merril Company, 1927.

Taylor, Lawrence Douglas. *La gran aventura en México*, 2 tomos, México, D.F.: Consejo Nacional para la Cultura y Las Artes, 1993.

Thomas, Lately. *Between Two Empires: The Life Story of California's First Senator, William McKendree Gwin*. Boston: Houghton-Mifflin 1969.

Thompson, Jerry (ed.). *Fifty Miles and a Fight: Major Samuel Peter Heintzel Man's Journal of Texas and the Cortina War*. Austin: Texas State Historical Association, 1998.

_____. *Juan Cortina and the Texas-Mexico Frontier, 1859-1877*. El Paso: Texas Western Press, 1994.

Torrans, Thomas. *Forging the Tortilla Curtain: Cultural Drift and Change Along the United States-Mexico Border, From the Spanish Era to the Present*. Fort Worth: Texas Christian University Press, 2000.

Vásquez, Josefina Zoraida and Lorenzo Meyer. *The United States and Mexico*. Chicago: The University of Chicago Press, 1985.

Walker, William. *The War in Nicaragua*. Mobile, Alabama: S.H. Goetzel and Company, 1860.

Weinberg, Albert K. *Manifest Destiny*. Baltimore: Johns Hopkins Press, 1935.

Vanderwood, Paul J. *Disorder and Progress: Bandits, Police, and Mexican Development*. Lincoln: University of Nebraska Press, 1981.

Velasco Ceballos, Rómulo. *¿Se apoderará Estados Unidos de América de Baja California?: La invasión filibustera de 1911*. México, D.F.: Imprenta Nacional, 1920.

Zorilla, Luis G. *Historia de las relaciones entre México y Estados Unidos de América, 1800-1958*. 2 tomos. México, D.F.: Editorial Porrúa, 1965.

Woodward, Arthur (ed.). *The Republic of Lower California, 1853- 1854, in the Words of its State Papers, Eyewitnesses, and Contemporary Reporters*. Los Angeles: Dawson's Book Store, 1966.

Wyllys, Rufus K. *The French in Sonora*. Berkeley: University of California Press, 1932.

Articles:

Blaisdell, Lowell L. "Harry Chandler and Mexican Border Intrigue, 1914-

1917." *Pacific Historical Review.* 35 (Fall 1966), 385-393.

_____. "Was It Revolution or Filibustering? The Mystery of the Flores Magón Revolt in Baja California." *Pacific Historical Review,* 23 (May 1954), 147-164.

Chamberlain, Eugene K. "Baja California After Walker: The Zerman Enterprise." *The Hispanic American Historical Review,* 34 (May 1954), 175-189.

_____. "Mexican Colonization Verses American Interests in Lower California." *Pacific Historical Review.* 20 (January 1951), 43-55.

Coleman, Evan J. (ed.). "Senator Gwin's Plan For the Colonization of Sonora." *Overland Monthly,* second series, volumes 17 and 18 (January-December 1891), 4497-519, 593-606, 203-213.

Flores D., Jorge. "La expedición filibustera de Juan Napoleón Zerman." *Documentos para la historia de la Baja California, papeles históricas Mexicanas.* 2 (México, D.F., 1940) 33-65.

Gerhard, Peter. "The Socialist Invasion of Baja California, 1911." *Pacific Historical Review,* 15 (September 1946), 295-304.

Hewitt, Harry P. and Robert Cunningham, "'A Lovely Land Full of Roses and Thorns': Emil Landberg and Mexico, 1835-1866," *Southwestern Historical Quarterly,* vol. 93 (January 1995), 386-425.

Hewitt, Herry P., "'El deseo de cubrir el honor nacional': Francisco Jiménez and the Survey of the Mexico-United States Boundary, 1849-1857," in *Ciudad y campo en la historia de México,* Ricardo Sánchez, Eric Van Young and Gisela Von Wobeser, eds., 2 vols. (México, D.F.: Instituto de Investigaciones Históricas, Universidad Nacional Autónoma de México, 1992), 709-719

_____ "The Mexican Boundary Survey Team: Pedro García Conde in California," *Western Historical Quarterly,* vol. 21 (May 1990), 171-196.

_____ "The Mexican Commission and Its Survey of the Rio Grand Boundary, 1850-1854," *Southwestern Historical Quarterly,* vol. 94, (April 1991), 555-580.

McPherson, Hallie M. "The Plan of William McKendree Gwin for a Colony in North Mexico, 1863-1865." *Pacific Historical Review,* vol. 2 (December 1933), 357-386.

Metcalf, Helen Broughall, "The California French Filibusters in Sonora." *California Historical Quarterly,* 18 (March 1939), 3- 21.

Nasatir, A. P. "The Second Incumbency of Jacques A. Morenhout."

California Historical Review, 27 (June 1948), 141-148.

Rolle, Andrew F. "Futile Filibustering in Baja California, 1888-1890." *Pacific Historical Review*, 20 (May 1951),159-166.

Suárez Arguello, Ana Rosa. "William M. Gwin: Su proyecto de colonización del noreste de México (1864-1865)." *Secuencia: Revista Americana de Ciencias Sociales*, 4 (enero-abril 1986), 134-142.

Thomas, Lately. "The Operator and the Emperors." *American Heritage*, 15 (April 1964), 4-23, 82-83.

Webster, Michael. "Intrigue on the Rio Grande: The Río Bravo Affair, 1875." *Southwestern Historical Quarterly*, 74 (October 1970), 149-164.

Wyllys, Rufus K. "The Republic of Lower California, 1853-1854." *Pacific Historical Review*, II (June 1933), 194-213.

_____. "William Walker's Invasion of Sonora, 1854." *Arizona Historical Review*, 6 (October 1935), 61-67.

_____."Henry A. Crabb—A Tragedy of the Sonora Frontier." *Pacific Historical Review*, 9 (June 1940), 183-194.

INDEX